Blacks and American Medical Care

Published with assistance from the Roger E. Joseph
Memorial Fund for greater understanding of public
affairs, a cause in which Roger Joseph believed

Blacks
and American
Medical
Care

MAX SEHAM, M.D.

THE UNIVERSITY OF MINNESOTA PRESS • MINNEAPOLIS

Library of Congress Catalog Card Number: 73-89963

ISBN 0-8166-0705-2

Part of the chapter "Health of the Black Child" appeared in
modified form as "Poverty, Illness, and the Negro Child" in *Pediatrics*,
vol. 46 (August 1970), no. 2, pp. 305–311, and is reprinted
here by permission of the copyright holder,
the American Academy of Pediatrics.

1809578

To *MITCHELL V. CHARNLEY*

FOREWORD

Max Seham appropriately begins his book with a quotation from Daniel Schorr's *Don't Get Sick in America*. The dire warning of Schorr's title is one of the themes in *Blacks and American Medical Care*. Several other related warnings are present too, although they are not always so succinctly stated.

Don't be uneducated, unskilled, or naive in America because the materialistic system tends to reward those who are most exploitative of nature and of their fellow man. To be uneducated, unskilled, or naive is to risk poverty. Don't be poor because to be poor in America is somehow to be less worthy. Don't be black in America because to be black is to be even more unworthy, and it tends to increase one's chances of being poor. To be poor in America is to increase one's chances of being sick. To be sick and poor in America is to increase the risk of dying regardless of age.

The concept of the right to health is developed historically as the book begins. That this concept is rhetoric rather than reality, not only for blacks but for all Americans, quickly becomes apparent as we are again reminded that there is no national plan or national health policy designed to fulfill this right.

In the United States racism is still a way of life, and the humanity of both the racist and his victim is diminished because of it. Internationally, we are thought of as "Ugly Americans" because of our racism and our exploitative materialism. Our foreign policy tends to accommodate more easily to material considerations than to human considerations. At home our materialism has permitted health care to be a commodity which is sold to the highest bidder. Only grudging consideration is given to the poor, who, as Dr. Alonzo Yerby says, are often forced "to barter their bodies" for health care.

There have always been those who have fought against materialism in health care. There have always been those who have fought against racism. To fight simultaneously against both evils is to champion unpopular causes. The author of this book has joined a growing list of individuals with the awareness that the problems are so interrelated that isolated or categorical attempts at solutions are inadequate. In his views the author has at times stood alone far ahead of his time.

Max Seham is a concerned, white physician who has elected to attack injustice and inhumanity on many fronts. He has fought to improve health care and attempted to break the incestuous relationship between poverty and ill health. In his concern for the plight of blacks as they struggle against the hazards of racism, poverty, and ill health in America, Max Seham stands apart from the typical American physician who works hard for his patients but is somehow blind to the fact that the harder he works the more he supports a system that does not operate to the advantage of all the people.

When the twentieth century dawned seventy odd years ago, Max Seham had already completed the first decade of his life. And now, approaching his ninth decade, he is in a unique position to assay the medical scene as he continues his fight, through this book, to improve the plight of his fellow man.

As I read this book and as I think of Max Seham, I am reminded of the words of Henry David Thoreau:

> The greater part of what my neighbors call good I
> believe in my soul to be bad, and if I repent of anything,
> it is very likely to be my good behavior. What demon
> possessed me that I behaved so well? . . .

FOREWORD

If a man does not keep pace with his companions,
perhaps it is because he hears a different drummer. Let
him step to the music which he hears, however measured
or far away.

Max Seham marches in the front ranks of those who hear
a different drummer. The information set forth in this book
is fundamental and valuable. It should be known to all Americans who are concerned with health.

John L. S. Holloman, Jr., M.D.

New York City
October 23, 1973

PROLOGUE: THE RUMINATIONS OF A TROUBLED PHYSICIAN

When a nation is as rich in money, talent, and energy as we are, when a nation develops as much new knowledge and new technology as we do, then that nation has a responsibility to ask whether it is providing the best possible health care to its people in a manner that respects their dignity and individuality and at a cost which they can afford.

And if this is not the case, then we have the responsibility to ask: Why not? And we have the responsibility to pursue this matter until we have a system of health care in which our humanitarian ideas are practiced on a daily and a personal basis.

> Senator Abraham Ribicoff, *Health Care in America*, Hearings before the Senate Subcommittee on Executive Reorganization, Part 1 (Washington, D.C.: GPO, 1969), p. 4.

This book is a labor of love and was written to satisfy an inner necessity. Writing it has been both a challenge and an adventure. It has been a challenge to my obligation as a doctor. As a practicing pediatrician for more than sixty years, I could not help but feel guilty about our high infant mortality rate that ranks the United States far below many other countries, a condition that has clearly been shown to be due to racial discrimination. Writing this book has also been an exciting adventure, a chance to help in advancing the humanitarian concept of social medicine. I have taken heart from the courage and will of 22½ million black Americans who, oppressed and disenfranchised for several hundred years, have never given up the struggle to obtain their basic rights.

Looking back over six decades as a solo fee-for-service practitioner of medicine, I am compelled to ruminate over the past and worry about the present and future of medicine. The revolutionary changes that have taken place in the science and technology of medicine have forced a change in the attitudes and the behavior of many of those in the medical profession. I came to the United States with my family seventy-five years ago by steerage. My parents escaped social injustice and came to a country that was flowing with milk and honey. When I first hung up my shingle sixty-three years ago as a general practitioner, people looked upon the doctor as holier than the priest; there was a saying among my early patients, "First God and then the Doctor." In those days the doctor was a man for all seasons. He was an internist, a pediatrician, and an obstetrician, all under the guise of a G.P. He slapped life into the newborns and ministered to the aged during their last breath. Being responsible for the total health of his parish, the doctor was ready at all times in rain or snow, night or day, to walk his route. He was not only a medical technician, he was a friend, counselor, and confidant. He gave relief to those in agony; he gave hope and comfort in times of crisis.

Sixty years ago the problem of medical economics was simple; the practice of medicine was then a one-to-one relationship between the doctor and his patient. There were no consultant specialists except for surgeons and for more experienced practitioners. Hospitals were used only as a last resort. Expectant mothers were sent to hospitals only when severe complications arose. The few known laboratory tests were done by the doctor in his office; the X ray was still primitive and not very reliable. For diagnosis the doctor depended chiefly upon his five senses. However, we were imbued with the service ideology. Our interest in the welfare of our patients was our uppermost concern. The Hippocratic oath was not mere parchment to be forgotten after graduation but a tenet the G.P. tried to put into practice every day. We believed that "reward of financial gain should be a subordinate consideration."

When I first started to practice it was not a very profitable endeavor to be a doctor. And later, during the depression of the early 1930's, medical societies actually maintained welfare funds to help indigent doctors in severely depressed areas. I never sent out bills in the early days because I did not expect to collect from those who couldn't afford to pay, and the others paid when and what they could. The fee-for-service system was satisfactory for both the patient and the doctor. The spread between the minimum and maximum charge was small: fifty cents to a dollar for office services, a dollar for home visits, and five dollars for bringing a child into the world at the home, with the help of a midwife, followed by daily visits for a week.

We were prepared to make great personal sacrifices, to wait out long starvation periods. Young doctors entering the practice of medicine at that time sought to emulate Dr. William Osler, not James J. Hill. We all started out literally as horse-and-buggy doctors. My first winter in general practice (in 1910) I walked my route with the help of streetcars, sometimes in knee-high boots borrowed from a fireman. It was two years before I was able to make my first payment on a second-hand car. A car in those days excited much curiosity, fortunately, for if it had not been for the help of a number of my patients' children, I would never have been able to complete my house calls — in exchange for rides the boys would get me started with a push (unwittingly, I encouraged truancy).

My ruminations about the past are now constantly overshadowed by worries about the future. The medical scene has undergone drastic changes, and with these changes the serenity and satisfaction of the doctor are undermined. What is happening to my beloved profession? In almost every magazine, in the cartoons and editorials of the daily papers, members of the medical profession are pictured no longer as next to God but as Satan's associates. We are held responsible for the high cost of medical care. We are accused of being more interested in minks for our wives and Cadillacs for ourselves than in the welfare of the people. For a long time we had the highest confidence of the people, but today we are suspected of betraying that trust for our own selfish interests. Beset on all sides by the hostility of responsible leadership in labor and criticism from high government officials, the ethical and dedicated doctor does not know what to make of it all.

Why this growing resentment toward the medical profession? Is it directed at the individual doctor, a certain image of the American Medical Association (AMA), or both? Is it because, having achieved upper-class social status, we have become alienated from the mass of people? Is it because in the last three decades we have become identified more and more as the prototype of the right-wing ultraconservatives? These questions are worrisome to a senior doctor who has always experienced the best of relations with his patients. None of these questions can be answered simply, nor are they based on myths. They are grounded in reality and are inseparably related to the many upheavals — scientific, economic, social — that have taken place in this century, and are still occurring.

To the public there has always been a clear-cut distinction between the role of the businessman and that of the doctor. Personal gain as a primary motive has long been accepted as necessary for the businessman; for the doctor public service was always to have priority over personal profit. Medical practice has undergone drastic changes since the new economic order of "free initiative, free trade, and free competition." Today the cleavage between the medical profession and the business world is not so clear-cut, and the gap is narrowing. In this age of commercialization it is more difficult for the private practitioner to reconcile his responsibilities as a social servant with his finanical goals. In a sense, the modern practitioner has become a small entrepreneur. He chooses a feasible location, invests his capital in facilities and instruments, and opens his business of dispensing medical services. It is inevitable that business methods will affect medical practice in a society that grants great prestige and rewards to the lords of finance. The result is a continuous struggle between two irreconcilable forces — service ideals and the profit motive. When I first began to practice medicine I tried, as did my colleagues, to live up to the letter of the Hippocratic oath. But living up to the Hippocratic oath and employing business methods are like trying to mix oil and water.

The modern doctor, especially the specialist, regards himself as a skillful technician, which he undoubtedly is. He is unquestionably more learned in the fundamentals of medicine than the horse-and-buggy doctor. Then remedies were largely placebos, now fortunately replaced by specific antibiotics and preventive vaccines. The modern doctor prevents disease, and cures people who in the past could not have been saved; if he is a general practitioner, he now has the support of more than thirty-five different consultants and an equally large number of trained paramedical specialists. But unlike a mechanic, the doctor is responsible for more than the repair of a machine. When a patient comes to his doctor, he comes seeking not only diagnosis and cure by the use of instruments and drugs. He comes also as a human being, and he brings with him moods, insights, anxieties, and tensions which the doctor is expected to respond to. The doctor should be as expert a sociologist as a technologist. But the fact is that scientific advances in medicine have come faster than sociological awareness; something precious has been lost along the road of technical innovation, expertise, and financial gain. Once a dignified and idealistic profession, medicine has been contaminated by the competitive ideas of business.

The watchword for the AMA over the past forty years has been, "What is good for the medical profession is good for America." Individually and collectively we doctors have fought, sometimes with vicious zeal, to protect and preserve our vested interests at the expense of the medical needs of the consumers. We have closed our eyes to the social and moral truth that health is not a private possession of the provider but a right of the consumer. For over forty years we were engaged in a senseless cold war with the government and other progressive forces over life-saving health legislation. This must cease if we are ever to attain an efficient national health system. Furthermore, in these days of rapid change, the horse-and-buggy methods of organization for the delivery of medical care must be abandoned. Just as we discard useless drugs and replace technical devices, we must discard our obsolete system of health care delivery.

The artificial barriers between public and private medical care must be eliminated. The shifting of responsibility among different levels of government must end. Where local communities through private channels are unable to act, states must aid, and if states cannot, the national government must assume responsibility. Just as the government has come to the rescue of sick industries and sick education, so must it help restore vitality to our sick medical system. The government has always played a beneficent role in protecting the health of the nation in times of depression and emergency. Society expects the government to assume more and more responsibility, especially in critical areas, and in fact, the medical profession has demonstrated neither by temperament nor by training that it is prepared to meet the social challenge of medicine, leaving a vacuum which the government should fill.

A quarter of a century ago I became painfully aware of the inequities and injustices in the administration of medical services when I confronted the restrictions of "Jim Crow" medicine in a black neighborhood house in Minneapolis. I sought the help of local government in establishing a free clinic for the black children who lived in that area but failed in my effort. For twenty-five years these children have had to depend upon the inadequate services of the county general hospital five miles away. Later on, my concern was kindled into anger, when as chief of staff of a private voluntary hospital, the executive committee opposed the admission of a black physician who was licensed to practice and who had a fine record as a medical student. This was the emotional trigger which compelled me to write the material which makes up the chapter "The Black Doctor." On re-examining the status of the black doctor, I still find the pervasive influence of discrimination — less than before, but still there. The last decade has seen much accomplished in eliminating overt discrimination, but there are still only a sprinkling of black youths attracted to medical careers; their situation is examined in detail in "The Black Medical Student."

And although I am a retired member of the AMA, and in good standing, I have pulled no punches in my criticism of the organization. There still exists a lamentable degree of social and professional discrimination on the part of white doctors toward their black colleagues, not only overtly but in subtle, covert ways. There are too many white doctors who perpetuate this policy or acquiesce in its operation; the conscience of the medical profession has as yet been touched only lightly.

We in the medical profession, with our heads in the sand, have refused to look up for fear of seeing changes in medical care which might lower our prestige and diminish our image. We have closed our eyes to the reality of the growing crisis. We have been a stone wall against which many health reforms have shattered. We have been afraid to innovate; we have been followers not leaders. Now, because of the seriousness of the medical crisis, we have no alternative *but* to innovate. We must not only catch up with the systems of foreign countries, whose morbidity and mortality rates are much lower than our own, but we must surpass them. I hope that time yet remains for our medical establishment to assert an unprecedented leadership in helping to solve the social medical problems of our time. There are battles to be waged against racism, moral and civic deterioration, poverty, and urban blight, all of which undermine our nation's health. We need leadership — wise, courageous, compassionate — we need medical statesmen, not medical politicians; social scientists, not technicians. We need leaders who are not afraid to tell it as it is — leaders who are not afraid to put the medical needs of the country above vested interests.

We must repent for our discrimination against black patients, black medical students, and black physicians that continues to be de facto if not de jure. We must once and for all time weed out the tenacious roots of racial bias so that no black physician or medical student will be denied human compassion and the opportunity to serve his fellow man, black or white. I appeal to my colleagues: we must all, as the disciples of Aesculapius, remember, more than ever before, to practice the philosophy "Man is nothing except what he is to others."

M. S.

St. Paul, Minnesota

ACKNOWLEDGMENTS

I would like to express my appreciation and my indebtedness to all those who in any way made this book possible. Personal friends as well as strangers, known to me only through their writings from allied disciplines, have generously responded to my requests for information from a wide variety of other sources. Black colleagues, various organizations, editors of journals which published a number of my articles on social medicine, a small number of congressmen and senators — all have given me invaluable aid through their respective skills. Whatever contribution this book may make to the elimination of racial prejudice in medicine may be attributed to their assistance.

The late Dr. Michael Davis, the Nester of American sociomedical economics, taught me forty years ago that "man is nothing but what he is to others." He crusaded almost alone against reactionary forces that considered all new health legislation un-American and a disservice to the American people. To him more than to any other person I owe a great debt for his sustained, sympathetic support and guidance.

Mitchell V. Charnley, professor emeritus of journalism at the University of Minnesota, my literary godfather, took me under his wing as a private student in writing and spent many hours gently reminding me that the first principle of good writing is to write simply and not talk too much; to him I have dedicated my book.

James Burrow, professor of medical history at Abilene Christian College, Texas, was of invaluable help to me in preparing early drafts of several chapters, and his assistance is gratefully acknowledged.

Although Congress has been slow concerning matters of national health legislation, it must be admitted that congressional hearings before the committees on health and medical care and the reports in the *Congressional Record* are a mine of information for a writer on medical affairs. Fortunately, there is at present a small band of congressmen and senators who are sincerely concerned and are dedicated to the implementation of the principle of the right to health for all.

I am deeply indebted to the librarians of the Bio-Medical Library at the University of Minnesota for going far beyond the line of duty in furnishing me with references.

I am especially obligated to Karin Johnson and to Aileen Cooper for the rewriting and reorganizing of the final draft. And I am grateful to Mrs. Mary Fryer, upon whom I could always depend for secretarial assistance.

Most importantly, I should like to thank my wife, Elsie, who put up with my engrossment in the research and writing of this book for three long years.

TABLE OF CONTENTS

Blacks and American Medical Care

THE RIGHT TO HEALTH

I've taken a lady to the office and stayed there until she waited on her, until she examined her. And before she put a hand on her, she said, "Do you have any money, honey?" And the lady told her she had some. The doctor said she wanted to know where she was goin' to get the money from. If you ain't got no money, you don't see no doctor. You just have to suffer it out.

Daniel Schorr, *Don't Get Sick in America*[1]

The right to health for every man, woman, and child was first expounded by Aristotle around 330 B.C. He wrote, "Health of body and mind is so fundamental to the good life, that if we believe men have any personal right at all as human beings, they have an absolute moral right to such a good measure of health as society and society alone is able to give them." This principle was carried out in ancient Greece by appointing state physicians to treat the poor. During the Middle Ages, feudal lords assumed the responsibility for providing medical care (such as it was) for their serfs, and with the rise of cities, charity hospitals, which had been the sole province of the Church, gradually were provided by local government, and, later, by central government.[2]

The attitude of early Americans was perhaps best articulated by Benjamin Franklin, who wrote in *Poor Richard's Almanac* that health of men and women is their own responsibility and that no one has the right to interfere with the individual's decision whether or not he wants health — a philosophy in keeping with the highly prized individualism of those times.

1

The best American expression of the concept of the right to health is found in Franklin Delano Roosevelt's new Bill of Rights. In January 1944 he said, "We have accepted, so to speak, a second Bill of Rights under which a new basis of security and prosperity can be established for all, regardless of station, race, or creed." Among these, he said, is "The right to adequate medical care and the opportunity to achieve and enjoy good health."[3]

By the 1950's medical care was no longer accepted as charity. Spokesmen began to demand medical care for the poor that was equal to that offered to the rich. With the creation of Medicare in 1964, which provided comprehensive medical care for those over sixty-five, the federal dollar began to be used to bring medical care to those who could not otherwise secure it. The expectation of comprehensive medical care for all, guaranteed when necessary by government, was beginning to be accepted. But much remains to be done. As late as 1967 Dr. Milford Rouse, then president of the AMA, stated that medical care was a privilege, not a right. He reflected a feeling that is apparently still shared by many physicians. An article published in the New England Journal of Medicine in 1972 provoked much discussion in subsequent issues which revealed a strong undercurrent of belief among medical men that no patient has the automatic right to be treated. Dr. Franz Inglefinger, editor of the Journal, replied to this discussion that "any person within the United States has as much right to health care as he does to adequate transportation, postal service, and fire protection." He goes on to say that "Without some ideologic as well as practical rapprochement, progress toward a generally satisfactory health-care system will be infinitely slow and painful."[4]

The Nixon administration has made no commitment on health as a right, but its drift may be surmised from a statement made by John Veneman, undersecretary of HEW during

President Nixon's first term. Mr. Veneman was quoted as saying he saw health care as being a responsibility of all levels of government, but "certainly not a right like freedom of speech."[5]

Today, under the medical system in our country — the wealthiest and most industrialized country in the world — there are millions of citizens, children as well as adults, who do not have access to good medical care simply because they are poor, or because they are black, or — most commonly — because they are both. This is not true in other Western countries, and the mortality and morbidity rates reflect the differences.[6]

Sweden, a country much like ours in its standard of living, found that those who most needed help were not covered under voluntary insurance and so, in 1955, they adopted universal compulsory health insurance. Although the Swedish Medical Society was not an enthusiastic supporter of the plan before it became a reality, indications are that doctors' worst fears were not realized. Commenting on the care provided for children, which is the aspect of the Swedish system that is most fully "socialized medicine," a Swedish doctor has said, "You can't make a business out of the health of children."[7] And yet we do.

Acceptance of the right to health principle is implicit in the British National Health Insurance Service started in 1948. The fact that the overwhelming majority of British people favor their system and the fact that it is backed by the major political parties[8] attest to the practical wisdom of this principle.

The British system asserts that the resources of medicine shall be placed at the disposal of all the people, rich and poor alike, in accordance with need and no other criteria. It further asserts that properly expended public monies for health constitute an investment which will give good returns in decreased morbidity and mortality, and in the prevention of pain and suffering. The fact that National Health Service (NHS) has become the way of life for the people and is the system accepted by the medical profession would indicate that government-subsidized national health planning is here to stay.

In 1970 I visited London and found that practitioners, though sometimes dissatisfied with their income and their working facilities, continue to serve their patients in the spirit of Hippocrates. One of the doctors whom I interviewed told me, "As a conservative I was vehemently opposed to the NHS but with time, as the plan seemed to be working successfully for the majority of the people, my attitude has changed and I am all for it. For the English people it has been a life-saving thing. Of course there are shortcomings, but we English consider the NHS one of our notable achievements. Politicians in this country would not dare to campaign against the NHS." One Conservative politician, a member of Parliament, told me, "You can cut defense spending, you can raise taxes, but you can never get along without the NHS. That would be political suicide."

The inequalities of the delivery of health and medical services in Britain have largely been ironed out. No patient now has trouble or great hardship in securing the services of a doctor for primary medical care. All English, Scotch, and Welsh citizens are assured of the same quality of medical care as that given to the wealthiest.

This cannot be said of the United States today. This country spends more on health per capita and more in total dollars than any other nation, and the rich can get the best care in the world, but as we shall see, the poor find it increasingly difficult to receive medical and hospital care. This includes more than half of the twenty-two and a half million blacks, several hundred thousand Indians, several million Mexican Americans, and the millions of poor whites who are below the poverty level.

I cannot agree with the laissez-faire policy still advocated by many physicians, politicians, and others who have the responsibility of solving the nation's medical crisis. This philosophy smacks of "each for himself, the devil take the hindmost." It is pure sophism to try to make a distinction between the social responsibility of the individual and the State in matters of health. If we believe that all have the right to reasonable standards in such necessities as food and education, why should they not have the same right to health? If the individual is unable to obtain health care through no fault of his own, local or state resources must be used; if local or state governments are unable to meet this responsibility, the federal government must do so. Fortunately, the pendulum in the United States is moving away from rugged individualism toward the more humanitarian principle of collective responsibility.

The purpose of this book is twofold: first, to present the pattern of discrimination against blacks in American medicine that has remained substantially the same for three hundred fifty years; and second, to record my experience as a pediatrician in rendering medical care to this deprived portion of the population in a large midwestern city. My personal observations are drawn from more than sixty years of medical practice — the last five of which included work with the Pilot City Health Center of Minneapolis which serves an area with the heaviest concentration of blacks in the city. This volume makes no claim to complete detachment because I have been mightily affected by the condition of the people I serve. Being involved as both a human being and a physician I have made no effort at times to conceal my emotion and anger over the injustices from which these people suffer. This book does not propose to deal with the scientific development of clinical medicine that has been adequately treated elsewhere. It is devoted, rather, to the problems of social medicine.

Racism, a recurring theme in my book, is substantially responsible for the poverty and medical indigency of most of the black population. Fair-minded students will agree that extreme prejudice signifies emotional problems in the individual and "sickness" in the society. It is not a genetic disease but environmental in the sense that many white children from their earliest years acquire the first symptoms of hate and fear from their parents. These are reinforced, and by the time they become adolescents it is often too late to recondition them to the truth that they are not superior because of their white skins.

Racism must also be considered as a public health problem. It may affect some 22,500,000 black Americans directly or indirectly. It is unique in that it has its most profound effect not on those afflicted with the disease, but on the mental and physical health of the minority groups who must suffer the prejudice of the diseased majority. It results in chronic inferiority, mental and physical, and has become perhaps the most formidable problem in social medicine today. It causes not only physical organic illness but it produces social, biologic, and psychological disturbances which keep the individual from living a normal and full life. In the case of poor blacks, these facts are confirmed by the actuarial tables depicting their increased morbidity and mortality and their increased vulnerability to illnesses of all kinds.

I can offer no better summary of the impact of racism upon the health of the blacks than to quote from a speech given by Dr. Chester Pierce before a conference at Portsmouth, New Hampshire, in 1969, when he said: "Racism is lethal by those who practice it and they may be guilty of murder, and those who permit it are guilty at the minimum of being accomplices."[9] He continued, "Racism does cause health problems in the ghetto. In a real sense it causes death in the ghetto. The parent of a child nibbled to death by a rat knows that racism played a major role in the child's death. The society that allows selected segments of itself to have over four times the general maternal death rate in childbirth must view its failure to that selected segment. When at birth the black child's chances, by virtue of his skin color alone, for a long and comfortable life are statistically different from the white child's, then racism is causing problems."[10]

As a physician I have been trained to think of problems in terms of diagnosis, prognosis, and treatment. Diagnosis consists of identifying a group of symptoms and finding an underlying process or cause to explain them. Prognosis is the process of describing what will happen to the symptoms or findings if something or nothing is done about them. And treatment is taking a course of action that will favorably alter the prognosis.

My diagnosis of the plight of blacks in American medicine, which is described in this book, is that today's medical system consists of a twentieth-century technology shackled with a nineteenth-century sociology. My prognosis is summarized by President Nixon's warning: "There is a medical crisis and if drastic steps are not taken in the next few years we are headed for a national disaster. There comes a time when profound and far-reaching events command a break with tradition, this is such a time — I say it because new knowledge and hard experiences argue persuasively, both our programs and our institutions need to be reformed."[11]

Agonizing though the process of change will be, the medical profession must come to grips with the business ethic; obviously, the doctor enters his profession to earn a livelihood, but the measure of his success should be the service he performs rather than the money he amasses. The medical leaders must accept the responsibility of leading this country toward aggressive, innovative change. In this book I have tried to document the reasons for the urgent need of such change. I have been given hope where I have been able to discover some changes already in effect; and I have pleaded my entire case in the faith that every citizen of the United States will join in a national effort to ensure the right to health for all the people in our land.

THE BLACK HEALTH CRISIS: POVERTY AND DISCRIMINATION

The notion persists that the finest medical care available — in fact, better than what most people can afford — is provided free to poor people in hospital clinics and even in private doctors' offices by topnotch physicians who allot a portion of their time to charitable work. According to a popular saying, you have to be either very rich or very, very poor to get first rate medical care.

But the poor know better. The most significant and unassailable truth, supported by raw and disquieting facts, is that the poor have a far higher rate of sickness and death in all the diseases that are preventable and treatable by good medical care. . . .

The truth is that sometimes excellent, sometimes shoddy, but always piecemeal medical care is delivered fitfully and distributed badly to the poor, under conditions that make a coordinated, personal medical approach impossible even for the most conscientious physicians. Moreover, these conditions are so surrounded with indignities and inconveniences that poor people, even when they are informed about the value of prompt and sustained medical care, characteristically come for medical help at the last moment — often too late.

Irvin Block, *The Health of the Poor*[1]

Every measure of health we have shows striking differences between the white and nonwhite population, and this gap is becoming a chasm in spite of all the advanced technical resources in our country. Blacks in our country do not live as long as whites; black mothers die in childbirth more often than whites and their babies are more likely to be premature, stillborn, or dead in their first year of life. Blacks visit doctors

9

less frequently than whites and when they go to the hospital they are more likely than whites to need a longer stay, which reflects the fact that they have been medically neglected.[2] In almost every category of illness, the morbidity and death rates among blacks are higher than among whites. Blacks suffer proportionately more acute and chronic illnesses. In 1960 the death rate for blacks from pulmonary tuberculosis was roughly four times that of the white population, and the number of active cases among blacks was three times as high. According to the Public Health Service data, in 1962 the incidence of reported syphilis among blacks was ten times greater than among whites and the death rate was about four times as high.[3] Hypertension, diabetes, cirrhosis of the liver, and malignant neoplasms also affect blacks more than they do whites. A wry comment on the status of the health of blacks was reported in a newspaper account of a meeting of medical workers on the health needs of blacks:

A black woman from Iowa . . . called to her fellow passengers not to hurry as they got off the bus that had shuttled them from meeting rooms of a conference on black health care to a cafeteria for lunch.
"Take it easy," she said. "Hypertension is killing too many black people."
Another passenger, darting out the rear door, paused and said, "And malnutrition is getting the rest."[4]

Black death rates relating to such communicable diseases as whooping cough, meningitis, measles, diphtheria, and scarlet fever are particularly high. This, of course, is because frequently black children have not been immunized. And in almost every category of causes of deaths for infants, the rate for blacks is 39.5 per 1,000 live births, almost twice as high as for whites (20.8). By category of disease, the rates are as follows:[5]

	White	Black
Infective and parasitic diseases	0.1	0.3
Diseases of respiratory system	2.4	7.1
Diseases of digestive system	0.5	1.6
Postnatal asphyxia and atelectasis	3.5	6.5
Immaturity	3.1	6.9

The difference cannot be attributed to income alone, since when the death rates of infants from low-income families are analyzed, race still makes the difference. The infant death rate for families whose income is less than $3,000 is 27.3 per 1,000 live births for white families, and 42.5 for blacks; when family income is between $3,000 and $4,900, the rate for whites is 22.1, and 46.8 for blacks.[6]

According to most authorities mental illness also appears to be higher among blacks than among whites. In 1950 data showed that there were proportionately about 33 per cent more black patients in mental hospitals than whites. In 1967 the incidence was not reduced. Whether or not the statistics on mental illness are accurate or, as some have charged, are racially biased, seems to me beside the point. More to the point is a statement found in a report of the President's commission that studied the effect of mental illness on our society: "It is no coincidence that in isolated rural areas and crowded city slums where the incidence of mental illness is abnormally high, there is also an unusually high rate of malnutrition, illness, unsanitary conditions, inadequate housing, accidents, lack of health care and education, and the pervading apathy of poverty."[7]

The reality of statistics on physical and mental illness among the black population of our country forces us to recognize the tragic outcome of a racist history of medical service. Martin Luther King stated that "Of all forms of inequality, injustice in health is the most shocking and most inhuman."[8] We must meet the black health crisis, for our society can become healthy only when all its members have been granted their inalienable right to health. Poverty and its resultant deprivation are inseparable barriers to adequate health. Despite the rapid social and economic progress of the past decade experienced by the majority of Americans, we still find that far more of the blacks living in the large cities reside in poverty areas as compared with whites. In the rural areas of the South, black sharecroppers are housed in overcrowded, unventilated, and unsanitary shacks. Poorly fed and medically neglected, they are highly susceptible to every kind of disease. Dramatic evidence of this neglect was found in the recent diphtheria and typhoid epidemics in Texas and Florida — sad examples of how our technology outpaces our society. In many rural and urban areas of the South it is common for poverty stricken blacks to die without any kind of medical care. We who do not see with our own eyes how severely deprived some of our fellow citizens are of even a nominal amount of medical care, find it difficult to imagine what conditions do exist. In 1968 Senator Ribicoff's committee heard testimony on health care in America, which brought to light facts such as the following:

A few years later I [Dr. Robert Coles] got involved in the kind of work I am doing now and I saw with my own eyes children suffering from rickets, and beri-beri, and scurvy, children who were malnourished, and who were showing it in their physical appearance, and who were fighting diseases that were vital to their very existence, and children who were born without medical care, and will live without medical care, and will do without medical care. They are children in the South and in Appalachia, but I regret to say there are similar children in many of our urban areas.[9]
· ·

All I [Dr. Joseph Brenner] have to do is to suggest to anyone here that they think about what it is like . . . to get up in the morning and have a minor attack of indigestion or a headache. . . . Now those are minor things, we take Alka-Seltzer for it. We rest for an hour or two, but they affect us, and affect us profoundly, as anyone knows who watches television. . . . Now, if we could only get the American public to imagine in their minds what it is like to live with excruciating bodily pain due not only to hunger, but due to the results of hunger, due to pain in the bones, pain of the skin, infections, suppurating sores or pus oozing out, all of these things. How do those people feel? What Alka-Seltzer do they have for their medical care? I think if we could only have the people of this country, the well-to-do people of this country see these conditions and know about them, then it seems to me we would have a different kind of uprising in this country. . . .[10]

But those hearings were in 1968, and current health statistics reveal no drastic improvements.

While the whites constitute the majority of the country's poor, the nonwhites feel the heavy hand of poverty out of proportion to their number. The black poor are piled up in urban ghettoes or spread out in rural slums where they live in overcrowded quarters with the most primitive means of heating and sanitation. Subsisting on inadequate, if not starvation diets, they do not have the resistance to ward off sickness and disease. Since the majority of poor blacks are inadequately educated, they know little or nothing about preventive medicine, which is one of the reasons too many black parents don't have their children immunized against contagious diseases. Often medical services are all but inaccessible. A 1971 report by the Health Policy Advisory Center states:

Not long ago it was commonly believed that sheer distance from doctors or hospitals was a problem only in rural areas. But today's resident of slums like Brooklyn's Bedford Stuyvesant, or Chicago's south side, is as effectively removed from health services as his relatives who stayed behind in Mississippi. One region of Bedford-Stuyvesant contains only one practicing physician for a population of one hundred thousand. Milwaukee County Hospital, the sole source of medical care for tens of thousands of poor and working-class people, is sixteen miles outside the city, and an hour and a half bus ride for many.[11]

Even though they may have access to physicians, hospitals, and neighborhood health centers, blacks still do not make full use of the facilities for reasons that will be discussed later in this chapter. The fact to be stressed here is that the health of the black population is a vital concern to us all — if not for humanitarian reasons, then because it should be understood that it affects the productivity of the nation as a whole. It has been estimated that the loss to the economy because of hunger and malnutrition is over 5 billion dollars a year; to end hunger would cost less than $3 billion a year.[12]

The fee-for-service American system of delivering medical services has failed to make accessible adequate health and medical care to the millions of our people who are trapped in the cycle of poverty and ill health. Data from the National Center for Health Statistics reveal that families with an annual income of less than $2,000 have four times as many heart conditions, six times as much mental and nervous disorders, six times as much arthritis and rheumatic fever, and almost eight times as many visual defects as those in the higher income brackets.

Poverty has many faces, all of them ugly. For the breadwinner it is the inability to obtain and hold a job for the support of the family. For the family it means being hungry and living in unsanitary, rat-infested, overcrowded houses. For the nation it is in social pathology what cancer is in physical pathology to the individual.

Americans seem to be divided on whether poverty is caused by lack of effort or is due to circumstances beyond the control of the individual. I believe current research in the social sciences rather conclusively rebuts an argument that want and deprivation are a stimulus to initiative and creativeness. In fact the opposite is true, that deprivation tends to stifle motivation. Generous aid and assumption of responsibility on behalf of a needy individual seem to create strength and security and foster initiative.

Blacks have always been behind the general population in

receipt of health services because of the practice of racial discrimination.

In 1964, before the enactment of Title VI of the Civil Rights Act, I wrote a paper entitled "Discrimination against Negroes in Hospitals" in which I produced documented data that discrimination was overt and blatant in all Southern hospitals and covert and hypocritical in the North.[13] The Civil Rights Act passed by Congress in 1964 was the most comprehensive and socially significant civil rights legislation since the days of Reconstruction. The Act included eleven titles of basic legal rights, including the one most pertinent to the theme of this book, Title VI, which provides in part as follows: "No person in the United States shall on the ground of race, color, or national origin be excluded from participation in, be denied benefits of, or be subjected to discrimination under any program or activity receiving Federal financial assistance." In very precise language Title VI refers to hospitals and all other health facilities.[14] Most of the nearly nine thousand hospitals in the United States are recipients of federal financial assistance. In addition thousands of health clinics, nursing homes, and similar health facilities receive federal money. Whether public or private, all facilities which receive federal funds are covered by Title VI and can be held accountable for discrimination in the use of federal money.

What has happened since Title VI has become the law of the land, a law which is supposed to give equal rights to blacks for medical care in all hospitals, health centers, nursing homes, and clinics which are dependent upon federal support? In order to answer this question objectively, I have studied the evidence that has accumulated during the past decade.

Before 1964 most Southern states segregated blacks in health and welfare facilities. In 1963, for example, black patients were admitted to the St. Dominic Memorial Hospital in Jackson, Mississippi, in a segregated ward. The obstetrical ward, delivery room, and nursery were on the second floor. After delivery, black mothers were returned to the first floor and their babies were segregated in a separate part of the nursery. Black fathers could not see their newborns because they were not allowed on the second floor. For another instance, in Atlanta, Georgia, blacks had access to 630 hospital beds out of 2,500 although blacks constituted about 50 per cent of the population.

The use of federal funds to build segregated hospitals in the South was bitterly opposed by the National Medical Association (NMA), the Physicians' Forum, and other organizations who repeatedly urged the federal government to withhold money from state agencies hiding behind the "separate-but-equal" clause of the Hill-Burton Act. This Act, passed in 1946, provided for the building of hospitals with federal funds, but provided also for separate-but-equal facilities, resulting in the exclusion of blacks from hospitals for whites. For seventeen years, the separate-but-equal clause was discreetly overlooked, and with few exceptions the public and even Congress did not realize that this item was really *separate but unequal*. Finally, after years of separate and unequal treatment of black patients in the hospitals, Senators Jacob Javits of New York and Hubert Humphrey of Minnesota took up the fight to prove that the separate-but-equal clause was unconstitutional. After two years of litigation in the lower courts and a final hearing by the Supreme Court, the separate-but-equal clause was declared unconstitutional in 1964. In the same year, the Civil Rights Act was made a law of the land.

Discrimination in hospitals has been ended in de jure but not de facto. In 1966 investigators from the Civil Rights Commission found violations of Title VI in some cities.[15] In Shreveport, Louisiana, the welfare office had removed the signs designating separate waiting rooms, but the room was divided by a solid partition with blacks and whites sitting on separate

sides. The director claimed that the clients preferred the segregated arrangement. An overt situation was found in the
privately owned Salem Baptist Hospital in Athens, Georgia.
Blacks were excluded from their services and the hospital administrator told the Commission staff he had no plans to com-
ply with Title VI.

Only 11 of the 39 hospitals visited by the Commission in
11 large southern cities, all 39 of which were receiving financial
aid from the federal government, had achieved any substantial
degree of desegregation in 1965, a year after passage of the
Civil Rights Act. A few had made some changes but had not
eliminated all discriminatory practices. In nearly two thirds of
the hospitals surveyed, there were discernible patterns of non-
compliance. No substantial change had occurred in patient
admissions or room assignments.

The Civil Rights Commission early in 1966 upheld the
criticisms by civil rights groups that the Department of Health,
Education, and Welfare (HEW) had failed to take the steps
necessary to achieve compliance with Title VI. In checking
over forty communities in the South, the Commission found
that only a few had proceeded to desegregate their hospital
facilities rapidly and completely.[16] At this time the Commission urged HEW to proceed immediately to cut off the flow of
federal money to hospitals and other health and welfare agencies where negotiations had failed to bring about active compliance. HEW, said the report, should also conduct *on-the-spot
investigations* to find out whether institutions were in compliance with the law.

The enactment of Title VI was a historic event in national
legislation, important not only as a specific tool to end discrimination but also as a symbol of the national desire to
redeem its mandate and provide equality for all its citizens.
But the rich promise of Title VI has not been realized as of
the 1970's. Based on a five-year progress study of Title VI

(from 1964 through January 1969), the gist of the investigations of the Civil Rights Commission was that discrimination still persists in hospitals and other health facilities — and the promised benefits of these programs still do not reach all disadvantaged Americans: "There has been too much tendency to compromise, to temporize and to use political tactics, rather than to be sincerely and forcefully committed to long range social goals."[17]

HEW had the pivotal role of responsibility for the de facto success of Title VI. Why did it fail to carry out its mandate to the people? Since the enactment of Title VI, there have been five secretaries of HEW, each with different approaches to the complex problem. The failure of HEW is in large part a measure of the failure of the entire federal effort regarding civil rights. Because of the many personnel changes, there has been little ultimate enforcement of termination of funds to resistant hospitals. Too much responsibility was left to state and local agencies. The result has been that in many states no compliance review has been taken and very few reports on the elimination of discriminatory practices have been received by HEW. Most of the nation's hospitals, including the 3,000 which only a few years ago practiced open discrimination, have not been reviewed since 1966.

In the absence of periodic follow-up studies, it would be premature to state that medical facilities have obtained complete and lasting compliance. Also, facilities in nursing homes have never been subject to review. All that can be said at present is that there is a difference of opinion among the HEW compliance enforcement officials as to what policy to follow to ensure de facto compliance in the future. HEW is also tremendously understaffed for the enormity of its task in reviewing medical operations around the country. It has yet to develop a format for evaluating programs in terms of their impact on nonwhites and in terms of their availability and utilization by minority groups. All in all, the solution is dependent upon a sufficient staff to enable HEW to carry out all its responsibilities effectively and not to reduce the effort to develop and maintain a comprehensive compliance review program.

If hospitals are to meet the needs of all people equally and adequately, past practices of racial and economic discrimination must be eliminated. As long as the bulk of our health resources are primarily financed privately and blacks are generally without the means to buy them, as long as health services which are publicly financed are not adequately supported, the quality of treatment guaranteed by law will remain a hollow promise. Without adequate enforcement of Title VI, many hospitals will be tempted to return to their former discriminatory practices. There is still a long way to go before racism is eradicated from American medicine. But defeat has not been accepted.

There are many different kinds of health discrimination, some still overt, but today most are subtle and covert. The circumstances, social and economic, in which most blacks find themselves are not conducive to seeking and obtaining adequate health care. The result is that blacks are likely to rely upon self-diagnosis and self-treatment instead of seeking medical assistance. In desperation they turn to the use of large quantities of unspecific patent medicines. In many, a chronic state of poor or borderline health is lifelong, and an irreversible condition is well advanced before professional services are brought to bear. Their chronic illnesses may range from simple dental caries to massive abdominal hernias. Centuries of neglect have bred in some a resignation to pain and a cynicism about what doctors can do. Dr. Coles has written about the results of his efforts to persuade a woman who had recently moved from the South to an urban ghetto to visit a nearby hospital:

Would not a complete and thorough medical checkup, followed by first-rate treatment, do away with those complaints, make her feel better, give back to her the good health she lacked for so long? Here is how she might answer those questions . . . : "I've been hurting all my life, and I don't ever expect to stop hurting. All day long there's one thing or another to put up with. When I was a little girl I asked my mother once if she couldn't do something that would stop my pains, and she didn't ask me where they were or how bad they were; no sir, she said, there wasn't anything that could be done. . . .

"A doctor, what can a doctor do to change our lives, even if he would come here, right here to our building, and give us all the medicines he had? Could we make him fix those stairs and get rid of the garbage? Could he help us with our children, so they could find jobs and earn the money they need? I don't blame anyone and not the doctors, not them. We never heard of them in Alabama, and we've been up here a year, and maybe it's real different up here, but it's not all *that* different."[18]

The careful, meticulous, and solicitous attitude toward health which is held out by the health professions and which is, by and large, subscribed to by the middle class often seems empty and minor to poor people, who feel they have more pressing problems.

For the most part, delivery of health care services is geared to the upper- and middle-class culture because these services take on all the qualities of a commodity for sale and the affluent are the preferred and often the only market. This is especially true in the preventive areas. Therefore, the priority given to health as a way of life by the low-income groups is far below the priority given to health by most middle-class persons. The dual system of health care delivery currently available in the United States creates a negative attitude among the poor toward the use of health facilities and medical personnel. The black health crisis can be met only if the reasons for the underutilization of existing health services are carefully studied and understood.

The poor have always suffered the consequences of the

deficiencies of our medical system in an exaggerated form. In a two-year study of the sociological and psychological causes of underutilization of health services in the lower-income groups, Dr. Anselm Strauss classified the nonclinical factors responsible as the attitudes of the white health professionals, the health education of the low income groups, the life style of the poor — that is, their social attitudes, the effect of discrimination, and the factor of poverty.[19]

Consciously or unconsciously, in the North as well as in the South, there are still many health professionals who display prejudices against lower-income black patients. Health professionals often complain that low-income patients have themselves to blame for not obtaining available health services. They feel that the patients are negligent and delay coming to the clinics and hospitals; that they ignore their children's symptoms until well advanced; that the children return over and over again with the same illnesses, such as diarrhea and nutritional disturbances, because the parents do not follow the prescribed treatments.

I have found from personal experience that it is not always the patient's fault. The fault may lie in the lack of communication between the family and the doctor. Instructions are often difficult to carry out because there are so many other immediate responsibilities. The mother in the family is often in a position where it is impossible for her to care properly for her children, especially when one considers that in the low-income family a father is often absent from the household. It is also unreasonable to blame the patients for continued nutritional disturbances when their economic level often prevents them from eating a balanced diet. White professionals should also consider the practical difficulties in consulting medical help. Many parents fail to bring their children to clinics because they cannot pay for transportation, or because, if the parent is working, it means taking a day off. The clinics are often not in the neighborhood and some lower-income people are so poor that even bus fare and certainly taxis are beyond their means. In the wintertime, without cars, it is almost impossible for parents to take their children to distant facilities; this delays treatment of such critical diseases as croup or convulsions or early diagnosis of pneumonia or meningitis.

Providing effective medical care to poor, and especially poor black, persons requires more than merely adding more money, more doctors, and more facilities. Merely adding to what we already have would not remedy the other complaints poor people have about their medical care, complaints which help explain the underutilization of medical care by lower-income people. For example, attitudes of many health professionals need to be changed. Like many other middle-class whites, white doctors think of blacks in stereotyped terms. They are irritated by the mannerisms and "foreign language" of blacks; they often do not hide this irritation. The patients, in turn, sense what the doctor thinks of them and may not return to the hospital or to the clinic. There is not much doubt that this kind of class bias profoundly affects both the quality and quantity of medical care received by these patients. Young residents may be well qualified in the clinical diagnosis and treatment of diseases, but they have had no experience in the nuances of human relations. Senior staff members go from one patient to another, giving clinics to students, often forgetting that the patient is a human being rather than merely the embodiment of interesting symptoms or an unusual disease.

In general, health professionals have little — if any — understanding of the life style of the poor. For a doctor to advise a patient who is living in poverty to increase his intake of protein, without helping him to work out how he can do it, is useless. Similarly, to suggest to a working mother that she come to the clinic for weekly treatments, when the clinic hours coincide with her working hours, is tantamount to not providing treatment at all.

During the four years I was involved in a Head Start Program and with the Pilot City Health Center in Minneapolis, I learned that if one does not understand the life style of the ghetto, one cannot hope to get the best results in diagnosis and treatment of the patients' physical and mental ills. Nor can one learn about the patient in relation to his total environment without the assistance of the public health nurse, the social worker, and the family counsellor. The doctor may never discover many related facts concerning the patient's state of mind when he comes for a routine examination. Information obtained by paraprofessionals in the homes of the clients is essential for adequate treatment. The more information the doctor has about the patient's way of life, the more understanding he will have of how to approach the patient. Most important of all, it makes the doctor see the patient as an individual and negates the stereotyped view toward low-income blacks.

Another problem that must be dealt with is the lack of *health education among low income groups*. Many patients are illiterate and superstitious. They prefer patent medicines, home remedies, or treatment by quacks. They are loathe to go to white doctors for fear of not being treated with dignity and courtesy. They cannot recognize early symptoms of disease because they have never been educated in the detection of illness. Black patients must be educated to understand the importance of early diagnosis of contagious diseases in children. Chronic diseases, which sometimes do not fully incapacitate or cause pain, warrant special attention in health education. Black patients must be alerted to the complexity of detection in such cases. Health education is a major component of preventive medicine. The Pilot City Health Center failed to make inroads in health education through the brochures and printed literature kept in the clinic. Very few mothers asked for or read the many pamphlets. It was our experience that only by person-to-person encounters could we hope to make a dent in educating our patients. Doctors and staff, given the time and the desire, can do a great deal in this direction; communication between doctor and patient is a necessary component of health education for the lower-income group.

Through the help of supporting staff members, I obtained a series of complaints from patients at the Pilot City Health Center which are exemplary of the general attitudes blacks have formed as victims of racist medical practice: "The doctors at the clinic get changed too often. I don't like to see a different doctor every time I go to the hospital clinic." — "At the hospital you have to wait too long. They have so many doctors who are just beginning to practice." — "Once I sat in the emergency room with my baby for seven hours before they even looked at her." — "The clinic doctors seem too busy to answer questions." — "When you go to an emergency room, the doctors are only interns and don't have as much experience as practitioners." — "At the clinic I feel I'm just another number and not a person." — "The hospitals today — you can drop dead before you can get help. They figure if you get there you are not so bad."

Obviously, adding to our present system more of the same will not remedy these complaints. Even if motivated to seek health care services, blacks often receive inadequate medical care which in turn lowers their motivation to use such services in the future. The black's view of medical care, certainly reflected in the personal complaints of patients quoted above, can be summarized as follows: care is (1) depersonalized and lacking in continuity, (2) devoid of a health professional with whom the family can build a trusted relationship, (3) fragmented, both with reference to the specific care to be received and the member of the family to receive the care, (4) often inaccessible, and (5) extremely slow in being administered.

Although it is highly important to focus upon financing and improving the resources and facilities for the delivery of medical care, in relation to the blacks, the Achilles' heel lies in the periphery of medicine: it is the lack of human relations between the providers and the consumers. It has been made more vulnerable by the traditional attitude that the health commodity is owned by the providers, the politicians, and the establishment. The conflict between the providers and the consumers is changing. The establishment has won most of the battles during the last forty years, but now the people at large have taken up the challenge to revolutionize their way of life.

All health agencies in any way responsible for the health of the nation — local, state, or national — must realize that the solution of health problems of the black is urgent and that an extensive national attack must be mounted today, not tomorrow. Technology and money alone will never cure this chronic social disease. The long-range program must include better education in health care, improved minimal levels of family income, improved housing, and the universal application of biomedical advances to benefit all black and poor Americans.

HEALTH OF
THE BLACK CHILD

In 1953 rats mutilated and killed an infant in an area next to the district in which I was working. In my own district they chewed the hand of a small black newborn infant named William Henry. William's mother and four siblings lived in a dug-out basement under a dilapidated row house. Mrs. Henry had been awakened in the middle of the night by the cries of her baby and found two huge grey rats on top of him. When she snatched him up his hand was a bleeding mass of mangled flesh. She took her baby to Cook County Hospital for emergency care.

Cook County, however, was more than an hour away by bus and in order to get there she borrowed money from her neighbors to take a taxi. Because she was afraid to leave her other four children alone at home she took all of them with her and they spent the night in the emergency room, waiting for the baby to be treated and admitted.

Bonnie and Vern L. Bullough, *Poverty, Ethnic Identity, and Health Care*[1]

It would be comforting if we could view the account quoted above as an historical anecdote, but the story of William Henry is still being repeated today in Chicago, New York, Boston, and poverty areas in other large cities. In the midst of the prosperity enjoyed by a majority of American citizens, over 25 million Americans belong to families with total annual incomes that fall below the poverty level. Of these, 10 million are children below the age of eighteen. An analysis of these figures by race shows that close to 40 per cent (39.6 per cent) of the black children in America and about 10 per cent (10.5

26

per cent) of the white children are growing up in dire poverty.[2] Crumbling tenements, inadequate sanitary facilities, malnutrition, and disease mark the presence of poverty. Public action has been inadequate to meet the total needs of families submerged in the economic struggle for a better standard of living. The children who through no fault of their own are compelled to grow up under these circumstances suffer from the "deprivation syndrome," a complex disorder which is often the consequence of severe social pathology. It interferes with a child's normal growth and development in the physical, mental, and emotional spheres. It may result in intellectual retardation, personality disorders, social maladjustments, and even brain damage. Although poverty claims victims among all racial groups, it has undoubtedly wrought its greatest damage upon the impoverished black child.

There is overwhelming evidence for a direct correlation between poverty and high rates of morbidity and mortality among youth as well as among other age groups. The maternal mortality rate is one of the most meaningful clues to the health status of a nation; the second most sensitive yardstick of national health according to the public health authorities is the infant mortality rate. In a sense, the latter is an index of what our society is doing for our children through the skills of our practicing physicians. Since accurate vital statistics are compiled for whites and nonwhites and since 90 per cent of all nonwhites are blacks, I have used the terms *blacks* and *nonwhites* interchangeably. Child or adult, male or female, a black in the United States is less healthy than a white. The first inalienable right, life itself, is cut short for every black child born; in 1970 a white male could expect to survive about 68 years, a black about 8 years less, and a white female about 75 years, a black 6 years less.[3]

A closer look at the maternal and infant mortality statistics of the United States gives a clear indication of the tragic dou-

ble standard of health care in this country. While the finan-
cially secure white mother can be assured of proper prenatal
and postnatal care, the poor black mother faces a much greater
risk of death for herself and her child with every pregnancy.
Trapped by poverty and prejudice, the right to proper medical
care is often denied to her. When I first hung up my shingle
over sixty years ago, the United States was losing about 100
mothers for every 10,000 live births. Today the rate has decreased to under 2 for whites but it remains about 6 for
blacks.[4] This can partly be explained by the fact that less than
1 per cent of all white deliveries take place outside of hospitals, whereas over 5 per cent of nonwhite newborns are delivered by midwives.[5] Pregnancy today holds far less risk of
death for all mothers than it did in 1917, yet the risk is still
three times greater among nonwhites than among whites because of malnutrition, lack of prenatal care, and prematurity.

Authorities are agreed that the chief reason for the high
infant mortality rate in the United States is the high incidence of immaturity and prematurity which, with the accompanying low birth weight, predisposes the newborn to the
respiratory distress syndrome within twenty-four hours after
birth. The mothers who have the greatest risk in regard to low
birth weight are the teenagers, the unmarried, and those with
the poorest prenatal care. In all these regards black women
rank the highest. Rates for prematurity average 5.3 per cent
for blacks of the highest socioeconomic status as compared
with 23.3 per cent for the lowest. The percentage is highest
among those with no prenatal care and lowest for those with
private care. Moreover, among premature infants who survive,
6 per cent of the nonwhites have congenital defects in con-
trast with 2 per cent of the whites.[6] These facts reflect bad
medicine, bad economics, and of course a low level of prenatal
care. Speaking at a White House Conference on Health in
1965, Dr. Alonzo Yerby described clinics serving the poor as

"crowded, uncomfortable, lacking in concern for human dignity, and worse yet, no longer free."[7] Such conditions undoubtedly have discouraged and frightened the black clientele. Conditions have improved somewhat since Dr. Yerby made this statement, but not nearly enough. Prenatal care is decreasing rather than increasing among blacks, partly because of the skyrocketing medical costs and the small number of doctors available. In inner cities the rate of prematurity has steadily risen to the level in 1967 of 7.1 per cent for whites and 13.6 per cent for blacks (which represents an increase over the 1961 figures) in the proportion of infants weighing less than 2,500 grams (about 5.5 pounds);[8] if the present low weight trends continue, we can expect about a 10 per cent increase in premature births in the 1970's over the number in 1967.

I have noticed that although the infant mortality is from two to three times greater than that of the whites in similar socioeconomic levels, the black children under one year of age whom I have attended at the Pilot City clinic in Minneapolis are much heavier, taller, and more muscular than their white counterparts. I have tried to find the reasons for my observation but can find no studies to explain why this is so. At all ages however, there is documented proof that a definite trend exists in the racial comparisons of height and weight; black children tend to be taller than whites and the white children tend to be heavier. Regardless of their age, black girls are equal to or taller than white girls, but at every age white boys are heavier than black boys.[9]

If we use Mississippi as an extreme example of what conditions exist in the South, it is a fact that not only poverty but discrimination as well are responsible for the double standard of medical care. If the same care were available to blacks in Mississippi and other Southern states as in, for example, Minnesota, death rates among black children could be sharply reduced. For example, in Mississippi in 1967, the fetal death rate per 1,000 live births was 17.4 for whites and 34.6 for blacks. Of the total number of live births among the whites, 0.2 per cent were attended by midwives, but 32.2 per cent of the black live births were.[10] In the same year, the fetal mortality rate in Minnesota was 11.3 per 1,000 live births for whites, and 17.2 for nonwhites. No white births and only 0.7 per cent of black births were attended by midwives.[11]

The infant mortality rate for the United States has decreased considerably since 1940. In the five-year intervals between 1940 and 1965 the infant death rates per 1,000 live births were:[12]

	Whites	Nonwhites
1940	43.2	73.8
1945	35.6	57.0
1950	26.8	44.5
1955	23.6	42.8
1960	22.9	43.2
1965	21.5	40.3

The sizable discrepancy between these figures continues: in 1968 the mortality rate for white infants was 19.2 and for non-whites 34.5; the figures projected for 1971 are 16.8 and 30.2.[13]

Marked differences also prevail in different parts of the same city. Recent figures for Chicago show that the infant mortality rate for nonwhites is 43.0 compared with 22.2 for whites. (For nonwhites living in poverty areas the rate is higher still — 45.5.)[14]

The National Center for Health Statistics has published a study revealing a "strong association" between infant mortality and family income; the educational level of the father and mother paralleling "substantial differences in the same direction as those for income distribution." The risk of infant death was found to be between 50 and 100 per cent higher in the lowest socioeconomic class than in the middle and upper classes. Exactly half of the black births but only one sixth of the white births were in the lowest income category. Mortality rates were

30

higher when both parents had an eighth-grade education or less; mortality rates in this category were 37.5 per 1,000 for white infants, almost double the rate for all white infants (20.8 per 1,000). This study was based on the National Natality and National Infant Mortality Surveys of 1964–1966.[15]

At the present time there is a pressing need for funds to speed up the attack against the high infant mortality rate among low-income groups. Maternal and Child Health programs, which provide prenatal and postnatal care, have brought about a significant decrease in infant mortality rates in the United States. Most of the reductions occurred in the inner cities (comprised largely of blacks and ethnic groups) which have maternal and infant care projects. If the budget requests are granted, in 1973, 152,000 mothers and 53,000 infants will be admitted to maternal and infant care projects compared with 144,000 mothers and 49,000 infants admitted in 1972. Since the programs were launched in 1964, 59 of which provide comprehensive care, the number of children hospitalized has been reduced by 50 per cent. This would seem to demonstrate that child health services which emphasize preventive care are effective among the poor as well as the affluent, among nonwhites as well as whites.[16]

Despite the improvement in both white and nonwhite infant mortality rates in the past three decades, as the richest nation in the world, we have no reason for pride or complacency. In 1950 the United States ranked sixth among countries in its infant mortality rate; in 1970 it ranked twelfth, with 18.9. As of 1972 infant mortality is higher in the United States than in many other countries. The U.S. rate is almost double that of Sweden and the Netherlands, where high quality State-supported medical services are easily accessible to all the people.[17] Why does the United States lag behind the Scandinavian countries, the Netherlands, Switzerland, England and Wales, Australia, and New Zealand in infant mortality rates? The best authorities do not believe that the difference can be accounted for by differences in definition or methods of data collection. The major problem with respect to infant mortality in the United States lies clearly in the high death rates among non-white infants.[18] In 1964, Senator Hubert Humphrey wrote: "If the infant mortality in the United States today was as low as currently reported in Sweden (14.2) and the Netherlands (14.8), there would be an annual increment of 40,000 children in our population."[19]

Since poverty plays a major role in causing these higher rates, any one of numerous plans could be expected to reduce infant mortality in this country. For example, a nutritional program for poor expectant mothers and for infants could save lives. Creative programs to train paramedical personnel to educate expectant mothers to the importance of prenatal and preventive care would yield large benefits. Of course, the most effective action to reduce the infant mortality rate would be to provide free medical care for all poor expectant mothers and for children up to one year of age.

Since the inception of the Head Start program in 1964 (discussed in more detail later), medical screening and referrals have shown that black children have many more undiagnosed and untreated defects than the whites. They have, for the most part, lacked immunization against contagious diseases. Furthermore, inadequate nutrition renders these children more susceptible to disease and less able to recover once they have become ill. Vigorous governmental programs of immunization can be carried out, although they are beset by logistical difficulties. Provided that the children can come to the clinic or that the clinic can somehow be brought to them, they can be innoculated against a number of diseases at once and hence be protected for years to come.

The problem of malnutrition is more complex. The need for many specific nutrients has long been known, yet there are children whose diet lacks all or most of the essential nutrients. According to a study published in 1970, 44 per cent of children in Sacramento County, California, whose families were receiving AFDC payments had gone without food for one or more days during the year because the family had run out of money. A study conducted in Washington, D.C., showed that of the 460 children from low-income families that were included in the study, 65 per cent of the infants between 12 and 17 months old suffered from anemia.[20] Studies run in other large cities yielded similar findings. One reason for this is simply lack of money; another reason is widespread ignorance about good nutrition. Advertising is a related problem — the snacks, sweets, and soda pop popularized for adults and children alike have no food value, but they consume food dollars and food stamps. Children are a prime target for such advertising, whether it appears on television or in the form of bright packages in stores. The cure for this kind of malnutrition problem is in the education of mothers and children alike as to the nutritional content of foods available to them.

But poverty is the biggest cause of malnutrition. Severe malnutrition during pregnancy has been proved to cause premature birth, increased infant mortality, permanent brain damage, stunted growth, decreased learning ability, and increased susceptibility to disease. Children of poverty pass through the growth period, when their need for all essential nutrients is the greatest, without even adequate calories. Dr. Robert Coles has written and spoken eloquently about children of poverty:

I saw widespread malnutrition in Mississippi. I saw it when I was examining children involved in the Head Start program. One does not see the final stages of malnutrition, the starvation that one sees in countries of Asia or Africa; on the other hand one sees a wide spectrum of diseases that are distinctly due to a poor and inadequate diet. Evidence of neurological disease and repeated infections that plague all parts of the body. Children with distended abdomens and a whole range of diseases that would probably shock the American public if they knew that they existed among American children, rare vitamin deficiencies resulting in insidious diseases like weight loss, muscle weakness, eye infections, loss of vision, infections of the mouth and throat, rickets, and skin diseases of all kinds. Marked chronic fatigue and bleeding of the mucous membranes caused by lack of protein intake. Also the whole range of psychological disorders like lethargy, despair and exhaustion.[21]

Unfortunately, what Dr. Coles described were not isolated cases. Senator George McGovern, chairman of the Senate Committee on Nutrition and Human Needs, has provided statistics that show that severe malnutrition resulting from poverty poses a serious health hazard for large numbers of Americans: "More than 14 million Americans have total incomes, including welfare, which virtually guarantee that they will be malnourished; 23.6 million more have incomes that put them in serious danger of being malnourished — more than 40 per cent of these Americans are dependent children."[22]

If we could ensure that infants, children, and pregnant mothers were adequately nourished, our country's infant mortality and prematurity rates would decrease. With this children would improve in growth and development, certainly of body and probably of intellect.

Caught within the cycle of poverty, malnutrition, and physical illness, the disadvantaged children of our country often experience the additional suffering of mental illness. The extent of psychiatric illness is impossible to estimate accurately, but it is likely to be more common among disadvantaged and minority groups simply because continuous discrimination and poverty may themselves be capable of provoking such a condition.

There has been much controversy in the last decade about the learning capacity of poor black children. Culturally deprived blacks have been classified as retarded because of low scores on standard IQ tests or poor records in school. The counter argument is that standard IQ tests are worded in a language that may be foreign to children from the ghetto and that the tests measure knowledge obtainable only from experience in a middle-class culture. In my work in the Pilot City Health Center in Minneapolis, where a number of clients had recently migrated from rural areas in the South, I often found it difficult to understand the language of my patients and their parents. Frequently I had to rely on my nurse to "interpret" for me. I can easily imagine the frustration of these children sent to schools where standard English is the lingua franca.

If a school experience is itself negative, the frustration alone could contribute to the emotional illness of a child. But almost no black families have the resources to obtain private psychiatric care, and public clinics and institutions are few and crowded. Thus, even an adult diagnosed as ill may not receive psychiatric care; certainly, there is little attention paid to early symptoms in children. Facilities are so limited that vast numbers of children requiring psychiatric help are never diagnosed or treated.[23] **1809578**

In a country as rich as ours there are too many undernourished children, whether from lack of food or the wrong kinds of food. There are too many crippled, be it from birth injury, accidents, or neglect. There are too many hard of hearing, too many partially blind who could be helped through hearing and sight conservation. Not enough schools have any child guidance programs for the thousands of maladjusted, insecure children. This situation is tragic in the rural areas and it is compounded among the urban poor and minority groups, especially the blacks. As long as we do not give greater priority to the application of contemporary technical knowledge, we must admit that our present health programs for children are neither efficient nor effective.

In the midst of this tragic situation some hope exists; what Medicare is doing for the aged, the Head Start program is attempting to do for the two million disadvantaged children of preschool age. The purpose of Head Start is to offer equal opportunity for every American child between three and five to get the educational, psychological, nutritional, social, and medical services which would allow him to develop his own best potential. The program tries to furnish comprehensive mental as well as physical health services to aid the children in mastering their environment. Head Start's rationale is that the children of the poor, especially the nonwhite, often begin school with a handicap stemming from their poverty which will retard their total development. This handicap may be psychological or sociocultural or physical. Head Start seeks to aid the whole child, preparing him not only for school but for his total life through health, development, and social services; it seeks to educate the family as well as the child.

The Head Start program was developed to use existing knowledge to help preschool children living in poverty, to help break the vicious cycle of deprivation of poverty's most helpless and potentially most salvageable victims — the young children. The project has not only been providing directly for the needs of children, but it includes the children's parents in every stage of planning and implementation. The parents in this way are supposed to acquire a new sense of dignity and worth and to modify their skills and attitudes in encouraging the development of their children. Head Start also has attempted to stimulate the local community as a whole by involving a wide range of individuals in organizations which plan and carry out the program. This confronts the members of the community actively with the problems of the poor and forces them to seek solutions to these problems.

Although the health aspect is only one of four services offered by Head Start, it has been given high priority in many units. The health goals of Project Head Start are twofold: To improve the child's present state by finding and remedying existing defects and to ensure the child's future health by providing preventive services and by improving the health of the child's family and his community.[24] The health component of the national program was first directed by a pediatrician, Dr. A. Frederick North. During the planning stage, the exchanges between the local programs and local physicians were often haphazard and lukewarm. Still, it should be noted that ten years before it would have been impossible for HEW or any other governmental agency to carry out such a project because of the opposition of the American Medical Association and the complacency of Congress. But strange as it may seem, when Head Start began, a government-sponsored and subsidized effort to promote the health of the young, it had the blessings of the AMA and most of the state and local medical societies. Although many felt there was some conflict between private practice and the government's activity, the prevailing opinion seemed to be that the program was necessary. Thus, Head Start yielded a side benefit by helping to improve the relations between the medical profession and families living in poverty.

The American Academy of Pediatrics has been in the forefront of supporters of Head Start. In October 1967, in order to have a close active tie with this worthwhile project, the Academy entered into a contract with the Office of Economic Opportunity (OEO). Under this contract the Academy agreed to "organize and direct the medical consultation program in nearly 2,000 communities throughout the United States."[25] It recruited, selected, and assigned consultants to review individual Head Start programs and evaluate their reports for OEO. Some 1,000 physicians, mostly pediatricians, were recruited and about 600 assigned. By 1968 Academy consultants were seeking to bridge the gap between local Head Start agencies and local medical societies.

In 1968, 800,000 of the more than 2 million eligible children were enrolled in Head Start. Dr. Hugh Thompson, in his 1968 presidential address to the Academy, asked support for sufficient funds so that every child eligible because of poverty might be included in Head Start. In response the heads of 94 pediatric departments of medical schools sent a representative, Dr. Ralph Wedgewood, to Washington to testify in behalf of the survival of Head Start. When the Senate offered an amendment approving the shift of the Head Start program from the OEO to Health, Education, and Welfare (HEW) to give it the institutional protection of a more established department, the American Academy of Pediatrics was concerned that many of the programs begun under Head Start would be discontinued and that programs geared strictly to education would nullify the project. As spokesman for the Academy, Dr. Wedgewood said, "The program should include parental involvement, health programs, participation by community groups and guarantees in the area of funding. . . . The amendment does not satisfactorily assure that nutrition, health and other programs, designed to meet the additional needs of children will be given supportive or consultative help."[26] Although Congress did not increase the appropriation for Head Start as much as the Secretary of HEW, Wilbur Cohen, requested in 1968, it did allot an increase.

At the end of 1969 about 2 million children in the nation had had some contact with Head Start programs for at least two- to eight-week summer sessions each year. Some of the medical findings for these first 2 million children were:

> 180,000 failed a vision test
> 60,000 needed eyeglasses
> 60,000 had bad skin disease
> 180,000 had anemia
> 40,000 had mental retardation or a learning
>   problem requiring evaluation
>   by a specialist
> 20,000 had a bone or joint problem
> 1,300,000 had dental disease
> 1,200,000 had not been vaccinated against measles

More than two thirds of these children received the medical and dental services they required through Head Start.[27] If an effort of this magnitude can be maintained or, even better, expanded, there is no question that at least the most severe medical ailments of children in poverty areas could be diagnosed and treated effectively.

Project Head Start is the most comprehensive program to date to meet the medical and other needs of disadvantaged preschool children. It demonstrates what can be done by organized effort on a large scale if adequate financial and administrative support is provided. But other smaller programs are also doing much to alleviate the medical problems of children in specific areas while at the same time exploring other means of bringing medical service to the ghetto. For example, one of the other provisions of the Economic Opportunity Act led to the establishment of some sixty neighborhood health centers in the largest urban slums not directly affiliated with Head Start.

One of the first neighborhood health centers sponsored separately by the OEO was undertaken in 1966 by the Tufts University School of Medicine under the direction of Drs. H. Jack Geiger and Count Gibson. The Tufts project is limited to low-income families living in a district where previously there had been no doctors or dentists. The health center is staffed by the medical faculty and by workers recruited from the community. It provides comprehensive, preventive, and curative care twenty-four hours a day (especially for infants and children), prenatal maternal care, and care for the elderly. "Basic to the program," says Dr. Geiger, "is the premise that health services should be comprehensive and coordinated, not fragmented, and that these services be made available to the community where the people are, rather than wait for people to come to often inaccessible hospitals. . . . "[28]

Another of the neighborhood health centers is a community-sponsored program to care for all medically indigent children in a geographic area within the purview of the Brooklyn Jewish Hospital. A special feature of this plan is to reach out into the community and literally draw in children who are in need not only of medical care but also of psychiatric diagnosis and treatment. Dr. Charles Pryles, the director, states, "We have got to see if people can be made first to want and then to demand medical service — if this experiment is successful a much larger number of medically indigent children who need but whose parents have not sought medical care will be rescued from much crippling disease."[29]

Another seriously impoverished area for which the OEO has provided family comprehensive service for about four years is the Watts suburb of Los Angeles. Watts is virtually all black, with an influx of about a thousand persons per month. Half the population is under twenty years of age. The health services given are part of a full program of education, medical, and psychiatric care and all necessary social services. In a survey of the children who live in Watts, it was found that 51.3 per cent of 1,135 children had one or more referrable conditions. At the time of screening 73 per cent were not under any doctor's care. Before the OEO plan was put into effect, attempts to secure treatment for many of these children were met with little success.[30]

I was associated with a branch of the Head Start program in Minneapolis as a pediatrician. The Head Start program there was first developed in 1966 under the auspices of the Board of Education and the Minneapolis Health Department under Title XIX of the Social Security Act. The Minneapolis Health Department provided screening and preventive services and corrective therapy to children enrolled in the Head Start program. Most of the centers were held in churches of all denominations and they were completely desegregated. Of the 997 preschool children enrolled, 813 received some form of health screening. One or more health problems were found in 63.7 per cent; dental problems were the most frequent, followed by defects of ears, eyes, nutrition, and heart. Of 804 children, preventable physical defects were found in 202 (24.8 per cent). Visual defects were found in 45 (5.6 per cent) and hearing defects in 76 (9.5 per cent) of 797 children. No positive tuberculin tests were found. Before the Head Start clinics, polio immunizations had been given to 15 per cent, smallpox vaccinations to 69 per cent, and measles vaccine to 79 per cent. After Head Start, immunizations increased to 86 per cent for diphtheria, 63 per cent for polio, 76 per cent for smallpox, and 79 per cent for measles. As of January 1, 1968, out of 813 children having a total of 770 abnormal conditions, follow-up care had been completed or was still being given for 550 deviations. Follow-up was incomplete for 15 medical and 107 dental cases because the children had moved away or their parents refused the services offered. In no instance was incomplete follow-up due to lack of resources or finances.[31]

A de facto test of democracy can be found in the sacrifices society is willing to make for its most precious resources — its children. If the millions of American children who are suffering from the "deprivation syndrome" are to have their inalienable right to total health, what is urgently needed now is not more conferences or more basic research but a frontal attack on poverty and its associated evils. Privileged American children have access to the best medical care in the world, but the poor American children get only crumbs of what there is to offer. The Head Start program still has a long way to go, but it has already brought diagnostic, curative, and preventive health services to more than 2 million children who had been neglected by their local communities. One of the most encouraging developments of the program is that not only have many teachers, ministers, social workers, physicians, and other professionals volunteered their services, but mothers and fathers of the children have for the first time become active volunteers. This humane social plan has revealed a reservoir of talented people in the local community ready and willing to contribute their efforts without pay.

Poverty, however defined, is the major barrier to the best medical care for millions of our people, black or white. But poverty is not a simple matter of having little or no money. It means also low educational standards, poor housing, and poor nutrition. The poor, and especially the black and other nonwhite minorities, have been trapped in a relentless cycle of poverty for many years. In this wealthy country, tens of thousands of black children get only fragmented medical care. The Head Start medical programs have at least cracked this poverty cycle by finding and attempting to correct physical, dental, and emotional disorders, and by ensuring the child's future health through adequate immunization. We have the know-how to save and conserve all our children. What we lack are public concern, a Congress that will respond to the call of social justice, and a new leadership of the medical profession that will cooperate. Why do the obvious and necessary changes in health services take so long in being effected? Why does an effective program such as Head Start constantly have to face the jeopardy of inadequate funding? In an age which prides itself on having mastered the technology of medicine, why does our sociology lag so far behind? We know what should be done and how to do it. If not now, when?

THE BLACK STUDENT IN MEDICINE

With public funds, the "system" has built a medical school in the state of West Virginia, whose population is 10 per cent Negro, which has graduated 2,400 students, including 35 Puerto Ricans, but only 2 Negroes. The "system" has produced Southern medical societies that still bar Negroes from membership. The "system" has permitted perhaps one but never more than two American Negroes to graduate from Harvard Medical School in any given year and has allowed virtually none to train for specialization in any of its 18 affiliated teaching hospitals. None has remained to practice in Boston, where the ghetto population has now reached 85,000.

"Medicine in the Ghetto,"
New England Journal of Medicine[1]

In the United States today, only 2.2 per cent of the doctors are black, whereas over 11 per cent of the population is black.[2] This state of affairs would seem to demonstrate clear discrimination against black professionals in medicine and, obviously, to call for an immediate and drastic increase in the number of black medical students, subsequently to be black physicians. That this needs to be done is finally becoming widely recognized. However effective this remedy might be, the fact is that increasing the number of black medical students is not a simple matter — largely because of discrimination of many kinds, at many levels, over many years.

Thirty years ago discrimination against the black medical student was both de jure and de facto. For example, in a midwestern medical school, two black students were admitted to study medicine. One, the son of a chauffeur, worked his way through high school as a busboy and waiter on a railroad dining car. The other student graduated from high school with very high marks. During their senior year of medical school both were assigned obstetric externships at the university hospital. When the two reported to the administrator, without taking his telephone from his ear, without asking what they wanted, he exclaimed, "Get the hell out of here, I never want to see you in my hospital."

They were referred by the chief of the department of obstetrics to the dean, who laughed off their story and told them not to worry — they could skip the externship and he would give them an A. They replied that that was not satisfactory, that they could not qualify to practice obstetrics with only a report card. The head of obstetrics, taking up their battle, told the administrator of the hospital that these two were fine students, their fathers were taxpayers, and if he refused them admission to the hospital, there would be trouble. They got their externships.

They encountered the same difficulties with the psychiatric externship, finally settling for a small hospital in a rural area because at that time only five hospitals in the state admitted black interns. In the end, they graduated from Meharry Medical School, one of two predominantly black medical schools in the country. Twenty-five years later, one of the students had become the head of orthopedics in a southern medical college and was awarded a Rockefeller fellowship in orthopedics; the other had become a highly respected and successful practitioner in a large southern city.

The experiences of these two black medical students have been repeated many times over. The first black American to obtain a medical degree was Dr. James McCune Smith, who got his M.D. in 1837 from the University of Glasgow. The first to be graduated from an American medical school was Dr.

David J. Peck, who got his M.D. in 1847 from Rush Medical College in Chicago. Gradually, other medical schools began to accept an occasional black student, but the majority of black physicians practicing over the last century have graduated from two schools, Howard University College of Medicine (founded 1868) and Meharry Medical College (founded 1876).[3] "As of June 1963 Howard had graduated 3,427 physicians in its ninety-five years and Meharry 4,261 physicians in its eighty-seven years."[4] And in the 1968–1969 academic year, over three fifths (61.77 per cent) of all black medical students in the United States were enrolled at these two schools.[5]

Segregation in medical schools has officially subsided over the past thirty years. In 1938–1939, 22 of 77 medical schools in the United States had black students; in 1955–1956, 50 of 82 schools did; and in 1961–1962, 57 of 85 schools did. In 1948 there were 26 schools in southern and border states that would not admit black students[6] — indeed, the only southern medical schools then open to blacks were Meharry and Howard. Of 1,258 graduates from southern medical schools in 1948, only 56 were blacks, all graduates of Meharry. This represented about 4.5 per cent of all southern medical graduates, although 25 per cent of the population in that area was black. The result was that "in the 1940's new medical graduates did not replace losses through death. There were fewer Negro physicians in 1948 (3,753) than in 1942 (3,810)."[7] After pressure from black lay agencies as well as from black medical leaders, reinforced by the Gaines and Sipuel decisions of the Supreme Court, Arkansas, St. Louis, and Texas medical schools first began to admit black students.[8] Among the 26 schools that excluded black students in 1948, 17 had admitted such students by 1964, and another 4 had stated that they would accept a black applicant "who was able to meet entrance requirements."[9] By 1971 de jure segregation had ended in medical schools.

This moderately optimistic picture is altered when one

examines the actual number of black students enrolled at the many schools officially open to them. In 1968–1969, 31 schools open to blacks had no black students; in 1970–1971, 21 of these still had no black students. The total number of blacks enrolled in medical school increased from 350 in 1939 to 588 in 1948 to 761 in 1956 to 858 in 1969 (see accompanying

	Predominantly Negro School	Predominantly White School	Total
1938–1939	305	45	350
1948–1949	495	117	612
1950–1951	518	143	661
1952–1953	524	191	715
1955–1956	525	236	761
1961–1962	595	176	771
1963–1964	542	173	715
1968–1969	530	328	858

tabulation).[10] However, in 1968–1969, the best year of the period, black students made up only 2.39 per cent of the total number enrolled in medical schools — and when Meharry and Howard are excluded from the total, only 0.93 per cent of the remaining medical students were black.[11] If the black population, over 11 per cent of the total in the United States, were to have been represented by 11 per cent of the students in medical school, there should have been 3,938 black students in 1969 rather than 858. The situation in 1971–1972 shows improvement: 4.8 per cent of medical students are black, but there still are proportionately few black medical students.[12] The reasons for this, and the steps being taken to eliminate it, are outlined below.

In order to qualify for admittance to any medical school in the country, a student must receive a satisfactory score on the Medical College Admissions Test (MCAT). Of 45,000 students taking the MCAT, between 650 and 700 are black; all of these students are of course competing for the limited number of places in the 98 medical schools.[13] Furthermore, black students, on the average, score lower on the MCAT than do white students. Reitzes found that the average black applicant accepted by medical schools had MCAT scores equivalent to those received by the average rejected white student. Some have suggested that this fact may be attributable to the nature of the MCAT itself. Bowers et al. have noted that "the greatest difference between Negro applicants and all applicants in performance on the MCAT is in the scores on Quantitative Ability. Possibly too much emphasis has been placed on the MCAT in evaluating Negro applicants."[14] And Crowley and Nicholson have pointed out that "most medical educators agree that one of the obstacles to the recruitment of Negro medical students is the inequity of using white, middle-class–oriented tests to evaluate black students. For example, the MCAT not only specifically measures verbal ability, but depends upon the individual's verbal skills in assessing his ability in other areas. Since verbal ability is influenced not only by home environment but by the quality of earlier education, those persons who come from underprivileged and opportunity-poor backgrounds are disadvantaged at the start."[15] And Dr. Philip Lee, former assistant secretary of Health, Education, and Welfare, has written that "the MCAT was an unreliable guide to performance in medical school or subsequent career performance. . . . the achievement of equality of opportunity will also require a change in the attitudes and practices of medical school admissions committees."[16] The MCAT test thus serves as a perpetrator of de facto segregation in schools where the admissions committee chooses to follow it to the letter.

However, many other admissions committees do give great weight to candidates' other qualifications — background, environment, interruptions of outside jobs, personality, the total qualities of the individual, and the student's drive and sense of commitment.[17] I remember one administrator remarking that if the school usually required a B average and they got a

47

B-minus applicant who had terrific motivation, they would rather have him than a fellow with much higher grades who lacked motivation. The real solution to this complex problem rests not only on the college level but below the medical school plane, at the elementary and high school levels. College records, the advice of premedical adviser, and personal interviews are also highly important. It is true that most medical students in this country do eventually graduate and receive their M.D. degrees, but the validity of the MCAT test as a predictor of the ultimate competence of an M.D. was challenged by a number of delegates to a Josiah Macy, Jr., Conference in 1968. Probably the most provocative and objective analysis made there was by David Johnson, director of the Division of Student Affairs, Association of American Medical Colleges.[18] In interpreting MCAT scores of individual students, Johnson reached some important and practical conclusions: First, the test scores lack absolute precision — for example, two applicants may actually possess the same abilities, but one may not do as well as the other on a given day. Second, relatively large differences exist in the average performance of applicants from various geographical regions — for example, the average verbal score of examinees from the northeast during 1966 was 551 as compared with a mean verbal score of 491 for applicants from the south central region — but that doesn't mean that in general those from the northeast make better doctors. All of these considerations should provoke greater flexibility in the decision-making of admissions committees, especially in the cases of black students.

The effort to obtain more black medical students has come about as a result of the civil rights movement, acts of Congress and court cases, and black militancy. Suddenly the black student has been not only accepted but eagerly recruited for predominantly white medical schools. M. Alfred Haynes has said of the situation, "If he is a brilliant and exceptional student, he may be sought after, courted, seduced, bought, and before he knows it, actually auctioned to the highest bidder in a fierce, competitive market of predominantly white schools looking for black students. For most black students, this will not be the case. The average one is more than likely to have scored below the fiftieth percentile in the Medical College Admissions Test (MCAT). His performance is likely to be below that of many other applicants to predominantly white schools. The educational opportunities at the school he attended are likely not to have been as rich as those of his white counterpart. All of this is the product of many years of educational disadvantage, which may have accumulated to such a point that by the end of college his chances of selection to medical school have been reduced academically to one tenth or less that of the average white student."[19]

The black college graduate is the veteran of many processes of selection. He is one of only 6 per cent of the college-age blacks who attend college — and more than half of these attend predominantly black colleges, where the dropout rate is over 50 per cent. But regardless of his native ability, an admittedly frequent problem upon graduation is "poor preparation in quantitative reasoning leading in turn to deficits in mathematics and inadequate preparation in biology, chemistry, and physics"[20] and inadequate verbal skills[21] — all skills needed for a successful performance on the MCAT. The quantitative deficits are probably partly the result of the student's years in school systems that could not afford laboratory equipment and teachers with strong science backgrounds — good science courses require a comparatively large, sustained investment. Blacks are especially likely to have attended such schools because of discrimination and the neighborhood school system in this country. A factor apart from the school system which may well underlie both quantitative and verbal deficits is the lack of motivation for the student to learn. Sustained motivation of this kind is often provided by the parents of the white middle-class student — from early grade school on, this student may be pushed to achieve; his parents' high expectations elicit a good performance, which they reward with continued support and encouragement. Such a background not only provides the white middle-class student with the knowledge he needs to advance further, but it provides him with confidence gained through successful experiences. When this supportive family background is coupled with schools well supplied with teachers and equipment, a student is prepared to excel on standard tests (prepared, often, by someone of similar background); when these ingredients are missing, a student's scores are accordingly lower.

The long-range solution to producing better-qualified black medical students, then, lies in improving the quality of education in elementary and secondary schools, so that he is prepared to take a solid premedical course in college and, in turn, to meet any admissions requirements, whether they include taking the MCAT or not. Meanwhile, in the continued presence of the MCAT and absence of adequate preparatory schools, a number of special programs have been devised to supplement the black student's educational background so that he can meet the present standards of medical schools. These include a summer program in English, mathematics, natural sciences, and social sciences for first-year students at thirteen predominantly black colleges; the Haverford year-long Post-Baccalaureate Program; and the Harvard-Yale-Columbia Intensive Summer Study Program between the sophomore and junior, and the junior and senior years. Programs of this kind, beginning with first-year students and continuing until graduation, could greatly enlarge the pool of blacks who might qualify for medical school. The special programs provide encouragement and practical training for the students, so that they become confident enough to attempt to reach higher goals than they might otherwise have settled for, and by specific emphasis on medicine, the programs interest a greater number of students in considering a career in the health sciences.

The most recent plan undertaken by Meharry Medical College reflects the determination of blacks to play an important role in developing such programs. Lloyd Elam, president of Meharry, has explained, "We are busy trying to increase the pool of qualified black students for all the nation's medical schools to draw from — working with black and white colleagues across the country. Meharry chooses freshmen undergraduates who demonstrate a high potential for a medical career — the first group of twenty to be recruited spent the past summer [1969] on the Nashville campus, getting supplemental instruction in the biomedical sciences. Each student received $500. It cost Meharry another $500 to keep and tutor each student. The twenty young students represented an investment of $20,000. . . . After they get through their four summer sessions, they'll be qualified as well as anyone else to enter medical school, perhaps better than many white students who haven't had the extra tutoring." Elam believes that for many black students, money is the most unyielding obstacle standing in the way of medical school admission. "Our students come from homes whose annual income is $4,700. These families obviously cannot spend $2,500 a year to keep a son in medical school. Right now this is a more powerful deterrent even than race prejudice." Elam is now engaged in setting up a national fund of $88 million under the auspices of General Motors. He is also conferring with other foundations for grants to support the original idea.[22]

With the same goal in mind the National Medical Association (NMA) has established a scholarship fund called the NMA Fellowship, Inc. It granted awards totaling $375,565 to 247 students, for study at sixty-nine medical schools during the school year 1969–1970. Howard University furnished 21 scholarships, Meharry 17, and the rest were from several white medical schools.

Dr. James L. Curtis has reported on the policies enacted by New York City area medical schools to aggressively seek black medical students. As a result of these activities, the percentage of black medical students rose to 5.3 per cent of all first-year students in 1969–1970, a sevenfold increase over the 1963–1964 enrollment. Although these figures are encouraging, they must be viewed as only a beginning, in light of the fact that close to 25 per cent of the population of New York City is black and Puerto Rican.[23]

Another means of increasing the pool of potential black medical students would be to recruit more black women. About 60 per cent of black college students are women, but less than 10 per cent of black medical school students are women.[24] If black women were actively recruited, the available pool could theoretically be doubled. At present, black women suffer double discrimination, by race and by sex. But Bowers et al. have pointed out that because black society is basically a matriarchal society, the black woman "may well represent a numerically greater source of physician material than her counterpart in white society."[25] A recruitment program for black women would have presumably not only to supplement the usual premedical education but would have to provide greater encouragement for women to consider a field outside their traditionally presumed interests. The black woman might have an advantage over the white woman, in that medical schools are eager enough to obtain qualified black students that they might put aside their usual reservations about female students. Furthermore, her matriarchical society may have supplied some of the extra determination needed to pursue a demanding career. Women's abilities in this area have been demonstrated not only by the successful female doctors in this country, but by the excellence of female doctors in the Soviet Union, where most of the doctors are women.

A problem besetting all medical students, whatever their race or sex, is the rising cost of a medical education. This cost now averages $16,000 for four years of medical school, in addition to undergraduate expenses; costs at Howard and Meharry have generally been lower than those at other schools.[26] Obviously, the cost is the most serious deterrent to obtaining a medical education — and in comparison with cost of preparation for most other professions, the cost seems exorbitant. Indeed, since medical schools must compete with other scientific disciplines for qualified students, both the high price of a medical education and the funds more readily available for other studies divert a number of potential doctors into other fields. There are relatively few specialized fellowship and scholarship funds available for any students, let alone the disadvantaged or black students who often need them the most. There are few black students who have the time, money, and effort needed to prepare for a profession long rooted in racial discrimination. Today the average medical student is about twenty-six years old before he has completed his formal education (assuming he has not served in the armed services). Upon graduation he continues his training for an additional year as an intern, and this usually is followed by three more years of residency to qualify as a specialist. He is over thirty before he can truly begin earning a living. Few black families can afford such an outlay; it is a greater obstacle to those whose families are barely able to survive on what they earn.

The small number of scholarships available are usually awarded on the basis of intellectual merit and economic need. However, many of the students in need of funds are average students. Also, these students need even more than full-tuition scholarships — they need "living expenses including spending money, so that the student can be a part of the social life of the campus. The black student has enough to overcome to be integrated into the academic community without the added burden of social isolation."[27] Many have suggested that the only source of funds in the amount required to make a meaningful improvement is the federal government. The task might commence with inclusive stipends for premedical and medical students.

The NMA has been a central force behind many of the changes in the status of the black medical student. Keeping in mind the inroads discussed thus far, it is of interest to take a closer look at the demands and goals of this black medical organization. The NMA conventions of 1969 and 1972 reveal an escalating concern over problems that continue to be solved too slowly for the satisfaction of many blacks in medicine.

At the 1969 convention young doctors and medical students calling themselves the Black Caucus presented a list of nineteen demands to the NMA House of Delegates. Following the recommendation of a special committee the NMA accepted fourteen of them. Some of these demands were as follows: that NMA take positive and forceful steps to get the nation's health professional schools to commit themselves to admitting black students in numbers proportionate to the black population of the United States; that NMA continue its efforts to organize and conduct nationwide recruitment programs; that no student who is admitted to medical school be deprived of the opportunity to pursue a career in medicine because of lack of funds; that the NMA lobby for federal support for all students so that discrimination against the poor and the black student may be effectively eliminated; that the NMA put itself on record in favor of eliminating the Medical College Admission Test (MCAT) in its present form as a criterion for admission to a medical college; that NMA demand open admission policies to all hospital staffs for interns, residents, and attending doctors; and that adequate health care should be accessible to all people at convenient times and places as a matter of right. Most of the other accepted proposals concerned innovative changes within the structure of the NMA itself, giving more power to the militant student arm of the organization.[28]

At its 1972 convention, the NMA focused its attention on black student admissions; it is now engaged in legal action to activate goals set at the 1969 convention in behalf of the black medical student. The NMA has proposed for the first time a Challenge Program to force legal action against medical schools in order to increase the number of admissions of black students. The new president of the NMA, Dr. Edmund Casey, has said the goal is for black enrollment to reach 12 per cent by 1975 (in the 1971–1972 school year it was 4.8 per cent). This matter will be taken up in the courts. According to Dr. Casey, ten of the worst schools from the standpoint of black enrollment will be selected and the United States attorney general will be asked to take immediate action. If this procedure fails, Dr. Casey said, "we'll have to take the civil rights route." He further pointed out that "the present administration is sort of not in our corner." Dr. Casey did not know which schools would be targets for legal action, but he suggested that Georgetown, Ohio State, Stanford, and Harvard were possible test-case schools.[29]

The issue of black enrollment in medical schools has carried a high priority in recent NMA planning. For several years the NMA sought to identify, counsel, and aid black medical students who were having difficulties in school; at the same time efforts were made to recruit more black student candidates. Although medical school enrollment of all minority groups has increased during the last two years, the proportion of black students has decreased to favor the American Indians, Orientals, and Puerto Ricans according to Dr. Emerson Walden, past president of the NMA.

The real test is not simply to enroll black students but to

produce medical graduates. Dr. Casey wants an all-out effort to prevent the student, once enrolled, from dropping out. The aim is that 12 per cent of the medical *graduates* be black. As president of the NMA Casey is establishing, as first priority for the society, a means by which this end can be achieved. He wants to establish a program, with money from the NMA foundations and the federal government, which would provide three months of preliminary training for all the black students in need of help before they enter the rigorous program of medical schools.[30]

In all of the efforts to recruit and assist black medical students, it is important to avoid a subtler form of discrimination. Although more than 11 per cent of the population is black, and a comparable percentage of the medical students should likewise rightly be black, black doctors need not necessarily serve the black population. M. Alfred Haynes has summed up the problem: "Many institutions are willing to train black students for the ghetto but other students are expected to enjoy a free choice. It is true that black physicians are providing much of the health care for the black ghetto, but the health of the ghetto residents is everyone's responsibility. Teaching institutions have an obligation to inform students of the complex health problems of the ghetto and to challenge them towards effective solutions. This obligation cannot be met by accepting a few black students and hoping that they will practice only in the ghetto."[31] Dr. John Norman, recognizing the achievement of having seventeen black students entering Harvard Medical School in 1969, has phrased the problem differently; knowing what has happened in the past, he asks how deep the new commitment to change is: "Will the Ph.D. in physical chemistry of this class be encouraged to enter a career ladder with upward mobility leading to faculty rank here or elsewhere? Or will he be diverted to 'a more appropriate ladder' perhaps involving some aspect of community medicine in our urban ghetto: Will he be patronizingly advised to pursue a lesser career for the 'greater good' while forsaking his own interests? Or, hopefully, will he be urged to follow the track of his choice, in the institution and community of his choice in a desired atmosphere of continued self-determination?"[32]

The pressures upon the black medical student to turn his thoughts toward practice in the inner city intensify when he applies for internship and residency. In the early 1920's, hospital staff appointments and internships for blacks were rare, in 1930 only 68 internships were available, and in 1939, 168. But new construction of hospitals provided 5,772 more internships in 1959 than there were medical graduates of all races.[33] This situation created enough demand for medical graduates so that a black student often was accepted at several hospitals, and the 165 graduates of Howard and Meharry in 1963 served their internships in eighty-three hospitals throughout the country.[34] That the situation has remained essentially the same is demonstrated by the fact that in 1968 there were some 14,000 approved internships and only 8,000 medical school graduates (the figure also demonstrates, of course, that not enough doctors are being graduated). On the other hand, discrimination persists in places; in Detroit, for example, seven out of seventeen hospitals had never admitted a black to their internship program as of 1966 and less than 3 per cent of all interns and residents being trained were blacks.[35] Discrimination in internships and residencies of course affects the quality of a doctor's preparation to practice, because a teaching hospital provides condensed experience with a far greater range of cases than years of practice ordinarily can. Although it has improved since the days when the two midwestern black interns had to settle for residencies in a small rural hospital, the situation needs much more improvement before it will be satisfactory.

After the expense of eight years of college and medical

school, the intern needs to consider finances in his choice of a hospital, particularly for a residency. Thus, black and white alike are often forced to choose an institution offering more money over another which might offer broader experience or better resources in the intern's specialty. As Haynes points out, "The economic pressures in the black community are such that scholarships and stipends often become a determining factor as to whether a student, accepted by two schools, decides to go to school A rather than school B. The same is true for the residency training."[36] He goes on to suggest that the selling of oneself in training could have far-reaching effects in future practice. Again, the possible solution is "direct federal support of all medical education and training." Another aspect of financing, both of medical school and of internships and residencies, is that it may have strings attached — in return for the support of his education, the doctor sometimes must serve a given community for a given amount of time, perhaps even in a given speciality. Some institutions are quite willing to admit a black student and to provide for his internship, *if* he plans to practice in the black community. All such stipulations restrict the student's and, later, the doctor's freedom of choice. They can also affect his attitude toward the practice of medicine, for it becomes a service exacted rather than one freely offered.

The importance of continuing education beyond formal course work is fully recognized. In order for a doctor to practice good medicine and to continue learning, he needs staff privileges at a good hospital where he can consult with colleagues on cases. But to acquire staff privileges can be difficult for a black doctor, especially since "hospitals do not at present have a satisfactory, objective method of determining competence. . . . Only too often, the black physician is assumed to be incompetent until it can be rigorously proved otherwise, when in fact, it should be just the opposite."[37] Even though strides have been made in recent years, the white colleagues a black doctor has to work with often still harbor feelings of prejudice against black physicians. Another means of continuing medical education is by participation in the medical society. Again, discrimination prevents or at least inhibits the black physician from keeping up to date, for blacks until recently were still excluded from county medical societies — and, hence, from the AMA — in some parts of the country. The problems black doctors face in obtaining staff privileges and membership in the AMA are discussed more fully below (pp. 71–78). The primary point here is that discrimination in these areas can affect a doctor's education as much as can discrimination in his formal years of schooling. Black doctors have through the years continued their education despite discrimination by founding their own hospitals and establishing the National Medical Association. But the fact remains that it is their right, and their patients' right, that black doctors be free to continue their education wherever they believe they can do it effectively.

Discrimination against black nursing students has followed much the same pattern as discrimination against black medical students. The first training program for black nurses was begun in Atlanta in 1881 because there was nowhere else for black students to go. In 1891, upon a black woman's rejection from a nurses training school in Chicago, Dr. Daniel Hale Williams founded Provident Hospital and its eighteen-month training program for black nurses. Others followed suit, organizing schools for black nurses in the late 1890's and early 1900's. Gradually, a few white schools opened their doors to blacks, but more usual was the story of a black woman who in the 1920's applied to the nursing school of a California hospital and received the following reply: "In answer to yours of June 11th asking for admission to our school for nurses, please note that it is impossible for me to consider your application. This matter was taken up some time ago and definitely settled. Trusting that you may realize that you cannot enter our school and with best wishes, I am, Yours very truly . . ." As late as 1941 there were only 14 white schools in the country that would admit blacks; in that year most black student nurses were enrolled in 29 black schools.[38] As of October 15, 1962, 165 of the 1,128 nursing schools still did not admit blacks,[39] and in Alabama and South Carolina no white school had ever had a black student.[40]

Despite these obstacles, the number of trained black nurses increased from 2,433 in 1910 to 5,589 in 1930. For many years since, there has been no accurate figure for the number of black registered nurses or black students in schools of nursing. However, in 1950, nonwhite nurses formed 3.5 per cent of the total nurse population.[41] There is no evidence to suggest that matters have improved any: the number of black student nurses admitted to baccalaureate and diploma programs in 1951 (an indicator of future numbers of nurses) was 1,350 out of a total of 41,667 — 3.2 per cent; and in 1963, 3.0 per cent of the students admitted were black.[42] In the same year, 1963, the Public Health Service's Consultant Committee on Nursing projected that by 1970, 850,000 nurses would be needed in the United States in order to meet the health needs of the nation; in 1970, the nation was 20,000 short of that goal.[43] Thus, the need for nurses and the relatively open admissions policies should make nursing a good field for blacks, provided that they can be encouraged to enter it and can have access to the financial and other support they may need to complete training successfully.

Such educational support would not go unrewarded. Bellinger and Cleland have reported that a greater number of black nurses remain active in their careers than do white nurses, thus making better use of their training and serving a greater number of patients. The net result is that "while it is probably true that the cost of recruiting and training Negro nursing students would be higher than for an equal number of white nurses, it is proposed here that the long-run gain in terms of available nursing resources would more than compensate for the initial cost increment. This argument would be expected to have particular cogency for those hospitals that serve the inner city areas. The Negro nurse would be less likely to flee to the suburbs once training was completed and would be more apt to accept employment in those institutions where the need is most critical."[44] Bellinger and Cleland found considerable interest in a nursing career among black high school students who were discouraged from inquiring further because they lacked either financial resources or the academic prerequisites for entrance into nursing school. Special programs could remedy both of these drawbacks, in much the same way that similar programs have operated in medical schools.

The education of black dental students, too, parallels that of black medical students. In the spring of 1970, approximately 2.2 per cent of all undergraduate dental students were black — 357 out of a total of 16,008. The first-year class of 1969–1970 included 3.1 per cent black students (136 out of 4,335), an improvement over the 2.3 per cent in 1964–1965[45] wrought by vigorous recruiting. Howard and Meharry enroll the largest share of the black dental students; in the past, this has been 90 per cent of the blacks enrolled, but in 1969–1970 it fell to 64 per cent, reflecting other dental schools' increased participation. The number of predominantly white schools with black students in the first-year class has increased from 8 in 1964 to 25 in 1969.[46] This progress can be attributed partly to private funding and partly to grants from OEO for "programs aimed at the recruitment and selection of disadvantaged students to the health professions."[47] Unfortunately, a number of dental grant applications approved for 1969–1970 were not funded, and there appear to be further cutbacks in the offing.

An excellent summary of the aims of a good program for black students — dental and medical alike — has been made by Joseph L. Henry, in an address to Harvard postdoctoral fellows in dentistry: "Identify the potential of Negroes. Admit them using the identification of potential rather than conventional tests which have not been proven valid for any minority group in this country, as noted by the American Management Association. After identifying Negroes with potential and admitting them, it is absolutely necessary to set up specialized programs which will make up for their educational and cultural lags. This action will have to be done in a programmed way. Students admitted should be extensively pretested and specific programs should be charted taking cognizance of the *adequacies* and *inadequacies* of the students admitted. Based on special screening and identification of potential in Negroes and special reinforcement or remedial programs, it will then be more palatable for great institutions such as Harvard to alter admissions standards for gifted Negro students. One immediate solution related to solving the problem in dentistry is to change your admission standards, not your graduation standards, but your admission standards. You must take into account the failure of your admission screening system to identify Negro potential as differentiated from potential plus cultural exposure."[48]

To produce more black dentists it is not enough merely to announce that a dental school will admit more black students. Dental schools have tough competition in attracting well-qualified black students, for other occupations requiring fewer years of schooling and offering equal or better incentives are all drawing upon the pool of educated blacks. Like the other health professions, dentistry must seek out the black student in high schools and colleges, informing him about service, professional, and economic opportunities in dentistry and about the scholarships and other aids available to prepare for it. At the college level, there is need for academic programs supplementing the predental curriculum and for financial aid to predental students. In dental school itself, compensatory programs, full financial aid, flexibility in the time taken to finish course work, and special encouragement are needed. All of these actions could increase the number in the pool of potential black dental students and, ultimately, the number of black dentists. The pool could be further enlarged by deliberate recruiting of the 60 per cent of black college students who are women. (At present, 1 per cent of American dentists are women of any race, whereas in places such as the USSR, Scandinavia, and Venezuela more than 75 per cent of the dentists are women.[49])

One especially persistent form of discrimination in all the health professions has to do with the shortage of doctors, nurses, and dentists among the black population. As noted elsewhere, over 11 per cent of the American population is black, whereas 2.2 per cent of the doctors, 3 per cent of the nurses, and 2 per cent of the dentists in this country are black, and percentages of black students of these professions are comparably low. These percentages reflect the extent to which opportunity has been denied black citizens, not only in these professions specifically but also in every area of life — the qualifications required of candidates for these professions can be met only by people who have enjoyed the benefits for which the American system at its best is known. However, many have interpreted these percentages to mean that there are ratios of 1 black doctor to 3,600 blacks versus 1 white doctor to 750 whites, and likewise for dentists (1:11,000 versus 1:1,750);[50] they conclude that to meet the needs of the black population, the number of black students in these professions must be increased. Implicit in this interpretation is separatism:

blacks should serve blacks, whites whites. The average income of the black population being lower than the average of whites ($6,191 versus $9,794),[51] blacks should serve a population largely without the funds to pay for adequate health care or insurance, while whites serve those who can pay promptly — even though blacks' educational and operational expenses are of course the same. The greatest needs among the black population being for general practitioners, blacks should choose this field over any other. In other words, blacks should subordinate their own desires to the common good of the community, whereas whites are free to choose their speciality, their community, and their patients.

The basic injustice of this attitude has been explicitly spelled out by Sell A. Dixon, dean emeritus of the Howard University College of Dentistry: "It is a false premise to continue to cling to the outmoded practice of equating the Negro doctor to the number of Negro population. . . . The Negro doctor always has and always will give his fair share of professional services to [the low-income] segment of our population. He most often is found to have sprung from this community; but the young, rightly, do not want to be bound by it or earmarked for it. The task of health care for all our nation belongs to all of us in the profession, and all must share it. It would be folly to believe that all elements of our profession would accept their fair share of the responsibility for the less affluent sector of society. Nevertheless, no special segment of the profession will accept happily being recruited and assigned, exclusively, to the sole responsibility for any ethnic or disadvantaged group."[52] And M. Alfred Haynes reiterates the point: "It is true that black physicians are providing much of the health care for the black ghetto, but the health of ghetto residents is everyone's responsibility. Teaching institutions have an obligation to inform students of the complex health problems of the ghetto and to challenge them towards effective solutions."[53]

James Curtis, in his book *Blacks, Medical Schools, and Society,* has given considerable thought to the problem of blacks practicing in the ghetto, serving their fellow blacks. He devoted a number of years of research to the question, Will the black graduates return to practice medicine in the ghetto? Curtis submitted a questionnaire to 25 black students entering the freshman class in 1969 and to 95 entering in 1970. The overwhelming majority of these students stated that they planned to return to the ghetto to practice. They were primarily motivated to become doctors because their people so desperately needed medical care. Curtis interviewed a still larger number of black students personally and concluded that they believed it would be a noble and altruistic act if they were to become general practitioners in the ghetto.

Dr. Curtis pursued these favorable responses a bit further. He felt most of the students would return to the ghetto because they had grown up there, *but* that once they had earned enough money they would move to the suburbs or other more desirable neighborhoods. Based upon his own experience as a practicing physician for more than twenty years, he had observed that very few of the local doctors lived and held offices in the heart of the deprived areas. As many as a third to a half of the doctors had their offices in the inner city but their homes were located elsewhere outside the area of practice. Most of these physicians had almost all black patients. Private office practice was often segregated. Curtis comments in his book that to train black doctors primarily so that they will serve black neighborhoods is not desirable: "it is most unlikely that black and white health care systems and markets can be maintained."[54]

These men have pinpointed the problem: black health professionals are being unequally held responsible for lower income groups, whether urban or rural.[55] It is time all profes-sional schools altered their admissions policies. Any institu-tion with limited places must select from among the students applying for admittance those which it believes can best serve the needs of the population. In the past, medical admissions committees have shown preferences for candidates interested in pursuing research or certain specialities over candidates inter-ested in serving the population more directly as family prac-titioners. In the future, it would behoove them to reserve a fair proportion of each class — at least half — for those students, of whatever race, who voluntarily choose general practice in the inner city, in rural areas, and in other areas where physi-cians are most needed.

But this is only a short-range solution within the existing system. The long-range solution to the shortage of doctors in low-income urban and rural areas lies in a double-gauged gov-ernment program: First, the construction and staffing of new medical schools and of additions to the present ones. A mod-est start would be doubling the number of places. A minimum of 11 per cent of these places should be reserved for black students at the beginning. Furthermore, a minimum number of places — say, half — should be reserved for those choosing to practice in specialities or areas where there is foreseeably the greatest shortage. Second, the government should deliberately encourage doctors to practice in specialities or geographical areas where there are shortages. This could be done by subsi-dizing medical education and by providing some means of compensation for practicing among indigents, rural and urban. This total program could best be carried out through a com-prehensive national health plan, superseding the present di-verse health programs with varying coverages.

Similarly, shortages of nurses and dentists might be met by government action. Again, particular care should be taken to guarantee that blacks have full opportunities to enter and practice these professions. Second, the health care of the entire population should be assured by encouraging all races to practice in a socially oriented rather than a technically oriented way.

Even further steps must be taken to provide adequate numbers of health professionals. More personnel are needed for the many duties which can be performed without a full degree. The present paramedical experiments can be used as models for greatly expanded programs to train associate doctors, associate nurses, and associate dentists —people who, after two or three years of post–high school training, can assume a part of the burden of supplying the public with adequate health care. Blacks who might otherwise be lost to the health field should be vigorously encouraged to enter these programs.

In conclusion, despite the end of de jure segregation in medical schools and despite conscious efforts in recent years to draw blacks into the medical profession, much de facto discrimination remains. This discrimination is rooted deep in past discrimination — in employment, education, housing, health care, and every other area of life. Thoroughgoing action is needed to eliminate what has become an ingrained part of the American system of education at every level from preschool on. The current effort to end de facto segregation in the medical schools includes programs for recruiting black high school and college students, providing financial aid, and supplying supplementary academic courses. These experiments are too young to have borne full fruit, but one can say at this point that the successful ones should be expanded and additional ones should be set up. When only 2.4 per cent of medical school graduates in 1972 were black,[56] there is decidedly room for improvement.

THE BLACK DOCTOR

That black physicians are being accepted into the mainstream of American medicine today with somewhat less resistance than in the past is an admitted fact. Whether or not this acceptance is coupled with the cordiality which is necessary to equate acceptance with welcome is yet to be determined.

Hubert A. Eaton, "Are Ghetto Physicians
Welcome to the Mainstream of
American Medicine?"[1]

The Hatfields and the McCoys, the feuding clans from the hills of West Virginia, are legendary. To Dr. James M. Whittico, Jr., president of the National Medical Association in 1968, they had real significance. His father, Dr. James M. Whittico, Sr., delivered "Mother" Hatfield's fourteenth or fifteenth child. However, Hatfield's son had to tie his father to a tree in order to permit the delivery. "Old Man" Hatfield was enraged when his son returned from town with a black doctor; he did not allow blacks in his house. Yet after a son was delivered, Old Man Hatfield had a change of heart and supplied the Whittico family with corn whiskey, chickens, and cabbages — anything they wanted was theirs. The black doctor received his due. But he had to make it into the house to prove himself first. Unfortunately, justice has most often been legendary instead of factual in the history of the black doctor within the American medical profession. Too many doors have been closed, and most black doctors have not been allowed inside to prove themselves and gain their just rewards.[2]

The treatment accorded the black doctor for more than a century by the American Medical Association and its component societies is a shameful record of social injustice in American medicine. More subtle and less publicized than that of discrimination in other social and economic areas, the record is a blot on the image of the medical profession. A study of this record reveals that those of the organized medical profession have turned their backs on the rightful demands of their black colleagues to get an equal opportunity to serve their fellow Americans, black and white, to hold full membership in medical societies, and to give adequate medical care to their patients in first-class hospitals. Moreover, the black doctor has been socially and professionally ostracized. He has been barred from the medical seminars without which a physician stagnates, excluded from medical conventions, and denied the right to become a member of a hospital staff.

Only 2.2 per cent of all physicians in the United States are black.[3] It has been estimated that there were 3,985 black doctors in 1932, 3,810 in 1942, about 3,800 in 1951, 5,000 in 1960, 6,000 in 1970,[4] and 7,000 in 1973.[5] The total number of doctors in the same period was 156,406 in 1931, 180,496 in 1942, 232,697 in 1950, 274,834 in 1960, and 313,559 in 1966. In 1942, 1 of every 3,377 blacks was a doctor, but by 1960, 1 of every 5,000 blacks was a doctor. Although there was a 46.7 per cent increase in the black population over the twenty years, there was only a 14.2 per cent increase in the number of black doctors — partly because, as discussed in the preceding chapter, the percentage of black medical students remained virtually the same. These figures may be contrasted with the fact that 1 of every 670 whites in 1960 was a doctor.[6] We may note in passing that neither ratio is likely to improve in the future because the capacity of medical schools remains substantially the same while the population continues to increase; only a marked increase in places in medical schools could change this situation.

It should be pointed out, however, that these figures cannot be interpreted to mean that every 5,000 blacks share a black doctor and every 670 whites share a white doctor. For one thing, many practices throughout the country are integrated, so that some black doctors have significant numbers of white patients. This is true even in the deep South.[7] For another thing, the geographical distribution of doctors is not in proportion to the distribution of the population as a whole. The nationwide ratio of doctors to 100,000 people was 156 as of 1966. But the District of Columbia, Massachusetts, and New York, respectively, had rates of 377, 205, and 219 doctors per 100,000 people, whereas Alabama had 80, Arkansas 88, Mississippi 75, South Carolina 82, and South Dakota 84.[8]

The distribution of black doctors differs from the distribution of all physicians in that a greater proportion of them practice in the Middle and South Atlantic states than elsewhere; the highest concentrations are found in New York, the District of Columbia, and California. In California, the number of black doctors has increased ninefold since World War II, and in Illinois, Tennessee, Mississippi, Oklahoma, and Texas, there are fewer black doctors than there were before.[9] These figures reflect the fact that the number of black doctors practicing in the South has dropped. The South has not proved itself to black doctors and with openings in the North and West, young black medical graduates have not been inclined to settle and practice in the South. A further phenomenon of distribution is the high concentration of black doctors in urban as opposed to rural areas and in the suburbs as opposed to the inner cities. And there are situations like that in Boston's basically black ghetto, where there are 80,000 Negroes, unemployed, underemployed, disenfranchised, hungry, and sick. In this area there are fifty practicing physicians whose average age is 66. Of the six under 50, three are graduates of nonapproved medical schools. Of the total number only 65 per cent of all doctors and 73 per cent of black doctors are directly engaged in patient care; the remainder are training, doing research, administrating, and so forth.[10]

In a comprehensive study of 4,805 black physicians in 1967, Dr. M. Alfred Haynes reported that 83 per cent graduated from Howard University and Meharry Medical College. Black physicians are less likely than white to practice in groups (2 per cent of the black, 9.5 of all physicians practice in this way). Some 39 per cent of black physicians and 23 per cent of all physicians are in general practice, 22 per cent of black physicians and 31 per cent of all physicians have specialty-board certification.[11] However, working with a smaller sample — 335 NMA members — George E. Schwartz and Montague S. Lawrence confirmed black doctors' propensity for solo and general practice especially in the South, but found 41.5 per cent of their respondents to be specialty board certified.[12]

Bearing all these facts in mind, I shall now examine the conditions under which the black doctor must practice. One of the biggest obstacles for the black practitioner has always been obtaining hospital privileges. S. S. Goldwater, superintendent of Mt. Sinai Hospital in New York, pointed out in 1925 the importance of extending hospital privileges to all practitioners of medicine: "It is to the credit of the open hospital that it brings into touch with an organized medical institution many physicians who, under a more restricted or exclusive hospital system, would be deprived of those helpful and stimulating medical contacts, without which they are in danger of deteriorating in medical knowledge and proficiency from the moment of graduation from medical school. . . . the open hospital affords far better opportunities for fruitful clinical study than can be found in the lonesome and dreary circumstances of private practice. . . . the actual treatment of the sick is influenced far more by mental habits formed by the physician after graduation than by the knowledge he acquires as an undergraduate student. The key to nearly everything that makes for efficient medical practice today is in the hands of the hospitals. Their duty is plain — they must open wide the door of opportunity, so that the entire medical profession may enter, for the fruits of medical progress belong of right to the many, not the few."[13] The value of hospital privileges is disputed by no one; they can continue a doctor's medical education, provide him with colleagues for consultation, supply expensive equipment and services on a shared basis — in sum, they permit him to serve his patients better than he might otherwise have been able to do.

Despite these recognized facts, discrimination in granting hospital privileges to black doctors has persisted for years. Lawrence Greeley Brown, who began his practice in 1925, described his own experiences in New Jersey: "Naturally, when the writer came on the field he sought to get privileges in the local hospitals. It is a strange fact that while the medical officials admitted that the hospital was indispensable to the practice of good medicine, the doors were closed to Negro physicians. It mattered not what his previous education was, it mattered not whether he led the board as two of my friends did. The exclusion of Negro doctors from hospital practice was the rule."[14] When Dr. Goldwater published his article stressing the value of hospital privileges in maintaining a doctor's medical competency, Dr. Brown asked him whether he had had black doctors particularly in mind while writing. Although Dr. Goldwater hadn't, he promptly took the matter up with the American Hospital Association; the Association pointed out that if Dr. Brown was "so interested in hospital practice, he should join with those progressive Negro Physicians, three of whom had already met with the secretary a short while before, asking him to lend his support to the building of more hospitals for Negroes. Thus, a timely movement was killed by a small group of men who had accepted the status quo without rebelling."[15] For years, black doctors had been building hospitals in an effort to provide services that were denied blacks elsewhere.

In the mid-1950's, Dietrich Reitzes and his staff conducted the first thorough examination of the black doctor's place in American medicine.[16] Although the study was limited to fourteen large cities, it did include more than one third of all black doctors and three fourths of all board-certified black specialists, so that the pattern which it revealed is probably representative of patterns of medical care provided by blacks at the time. In developing generalizations about the factors which influence the patterns of blacks in medicine, Reitzes found that the most important single factor determining the kind of medical care that black doctors could provide was the opportunity they had for continued education through hospital affiliation. This factor depended on (a) the number of predominantly white hospitals having black doctors on their staffs, (b) the participation of influential citizens in groups actively interested in integration, (c) the opportunities for black doctors to establish professional ties with white doctors, (d) the supply of well-qualified black doctors, and (e) the professional relations among black doctors in the community. Clearly, a number of these items are interrelated. For example, the number of predominantly white hospitals with black staff members was probably affected by community interest in integration, by professional ties between black and white doctors, and by the supply of well-qualified black doctors, but it is difficult for doctors to form professional ties when they never see each other at hospitals or meetings of the county medical society, and it is difficult to maintain professional qualifications of a high level without hospital affiliation.

Part of the problem of obtaining staff privileges lies in the fact that hospitals did not in the past and even in 1970 still did not have an objective method of determining competency. As Dr. Haynes has pointed out, "some hospital boards still exclude black physicians more on the basis of race than on competence. Black physicians would have no reasonable objection if the same standards were objectively applied to all. Consumers are rightly confused when a physician is considered competent to practice in one hospital but not in another. If a physician is certified by his specialty board or by the American Academy of General Practice, he should be assumed competent to practice in any hospital. This should include university hospitals, some of which are now the exclusive domain of faculty members."[17]

This problem was faced squarely for years by the NMA, which repeatedly asked the AMA to come to terms on hospital staff privileges and membership eligibility in state and county medical societies. By 1963, the fruitlessness of these efforts led the NMA to join the NAACP and the Urban League in accumulating examples of discrimination in hospitals and medical societies for recourse to the courts. But it continued to apply pressure on the AMA, and in 1968, the AMA outlawed racial bars to membership in its state and local affiliates. Thereafter, a liaison committee of NMA and AMA members was established to watch over hospital privileges and memberships in local and state medical societies.

Meanwhile, action affecting hospital staff privileges was being taken by other agents in the 1960's. Recognizing the enormous gap between the number of Americans needing hospitalization and the number of hospital beds available, Congress had passed the Hill-Burton Act in 1946. The Act provided for the building of hospitals throughout the country with federal funds, but discreetly permitted the hospitals thus built to exclude both black patients and black doctors. Because of the persistent charges by many organizations — black and white — that black doctors were denied staff privileges and that black patients were refused admittance or segregated during their stay, the Civil Rights Commission launched an investigation in 1960. That investigation recorded officially what had long been known: blacks were denied access to or segregated in many hospitals and facilities that received federal funds. As I have said earlier, after subsequent unsuccessful congressional attempts to repeal the separate-but-equal clause of the Hill-Burton Act, it was finally struck down by the Supreme Court in 1964. The Court's interpretation was ratified by Congress in Title VI of the Civil Rights Act of 1964. The decision did not end racial discrimination in health care, but it did open the door for legal attacks on discrimination in hospitals built with Hill-Burton money. Both the Court's decision and the Civil Rights Act clearly would apply to the black doctor's relation with hospitals — the ability to obtain staff privileges, the extent of those privileges when obtained, and the kind of treatment proffered the doctor's patients. We shall see, then, how much effect the two have had.

In October 1968 the *Medical Tribune* conducted a survey and learned that some progress toward integration had been made since Title VI of the Civil Rights Act had been passed.[18] At the time of its passage in 1964, Louisiana had the reputation of being among the worst areas in the country from the standpoint of the black doctor. No medical society in the state admitted blacks. In New Orleans there were no black M.D.'s in public hospitals. Applications for staff privileges in tax-supported New Orleans hospitals were turned down because membership in the local medical societies was required. By 1968, according to Dr. William R. Adams, there had been some improvement in New Orleans. Two of the largest hospitals had been opened to black doctors, although he noted that "tokenism persisted in the integration of most hospital staffs, and . . . the problem remains 'touchy.' " According to the *Tribune* survey, vestiges of the past remained in New Orleans in the failure of some private and state hospitals to add black physicians to their staffs and in their refusal to allow blacks to be inpatients in some of these hospitals.

In Mississippi there had been some overall improvement, especially in the attitude of the white M.D.'s who controlled medicine in the state. Dr. Albert Britton of Jackson told the *Medical Tribune* that the University of Mississippi School of Medicine admitted a few black students, but that discrimination continued "even under Medicare and in Hill-Burton hospitals."

The situation was reported to be similar in Texas. There was some evidence that developments had improved the lot of the black doctors, but problems continued to exist. According to Dr. Edward Sprott, Jr., there were subtle forms of discrimination and an "overt form of bias in the reluctance of most white physicians to assist a Negro in surgical procedures. . . . The process of integration goes on, but not voluntarily."

Dr. Arthur Coleman, a San Francisco physician, said that a common grievance of black physicians is that although they are accepted into medical societies in the North, they do not reach a decision-making level. "The young black medical graduate is well-trained," said Dr. Coleman, "and in many instances is a specialist. He wants the same rights as the white M.D."

The consensus of the *Tribune* survey seemed to be that while gains had been made since the enactment of Title VI, in 1968 it was "still not hard to recognize the field."

Although there is no clear consensus on the situation of black doctors since Civil Rights legislation, the majority opinion based on first-hand experience was summed up by Dr. Arthur Swan in his presidential address before the NMA in 1967: "When my white friends around the country say conditions are much better now, I usually point out two very significant things: (1) that there is very little voluntary de-segregation, and (2) the number of opportunities for intern-ships and residencies that now exist for Blacks comes from the tremendous shortage in hospital personnel — in many pockets of prejudice the acceptance of Blacks into the fraternity of medicine is moving slowly, too slowly, to satisfy the health needs of the vast majority of Blacks."[19]

It is quite obvious, then, that a wide gap existed between de jure and de facto opportunities for the black doctor to practice in full equality with white doctors. Generally, blacks have been granted only courtesy staff privileges. As Holloman and Swan pointed out, there are reasons for pessimism among many black leaders in American medicine. In order to obtain staff privileges, black doctors are required to wait out the same time period as a new physician, even though they may have been established in practice in the community for years. Many hospitals, especially in the South, overtly or covertly, arrange rotating assignments to emergency room duty to avoid or mini-mize the opportunity for black physicians to treat white pa-tients, particularly females. Because of the many handicaps in securing and advancing staff privileges in the larger hospitals, they have had to take refuge in smaller, less adequate facilities without the benefit of a formalized training program.

One of the most severe handicaps for the black doctor has been the traditional social structure of white medical societies which makes it almost impossible for the black M.D. to be-come an accepted part of the socializing and the policy-making decisions in medical societies. For over seventy-five years now, two separate medical societies have existed: the AMA, the voice of organized medicine consisting of fifty-four autonomous state societies which have had a long history of discrimination against the blacks, and the NMA, an organization of black doc-tors originally formed because the AMA did not grant mem-bership to blacks.

As early as 1869, three well-trained professionally eligible black faculty members of the Howard Medical School applied for membership to the local branch of the AMA. They were flatly refused. Upon being turned down they attempted to bring their applications to the annual convention of the AMA in 1870; they were rejected again. They tried for a number of years until they finally abandoned their efforts in 1884. By the year 1895 they had organized an all-black medical society; this was the official birth of the NMA. Unwittingly perhaps, Booker T. Washington's admonition in 1895 — that the races should be separate — led to a deeper gap between the blacks and the whites.

The separationists and the integrationists are still battling today. Unfortunately, the evidence of the 1970's still shows America to be an apartheid society to a great extent. The two national medical societies, the AMA and the NMA, despite changes in policy, remain essentially separate and not yet equal power blocs. Each society publishes its own journal of medicine, the extremely powerful *Journal of the American Medical Association*, with a tightly controlled editorial policy, and the *National Medical Association Journal*, which was established in 1908 as a forum for freedom of expression and an entering wedge into the mainstream of medical politics.

From its initial 12 black physicians, the NMA has grown to about 5,500 members enrolled in some seventy constituent societies; 90 per cent of the membership is black. The NMA has become a militant humanitarian force crusading not only for the black poor, but also for the Indians, Mexicans, Puerto Ricans, Appalachians — for the poor of all ethnic groups. Most of the NMA members received their bachelor's degrees from predominantly black colleges and their medical degrees from Meharry and Howard Medical Schools. Most of the members today have active staff privileges at a hospital; some also belong to the AMA.

After all the years of distrust and fear on the part of black doctors, and the refusal of white doctors to give blacks equal social and professional status, it is at last, in 1973, difficult to find a white medical society that absolutely refuses membership to blacks. Dr. James Curtis has noted that, ironically, the situation now is that racial attitudes have come full circle and it is the whites who find it difficult to become fully respected members of the NMA. An increasing number of white liberal doctors have joined the NMA, but they have yet to receive a total welcome. As of today they are tolerated much in the same way the blacks were tolerated after the 1964 Civil Rights Act was passed.[20]

There have been definite improvements in the relations between the AMA and the NMA despite the inherent fear and distrust among many whites and blacks. In 1968 the AMA finally joined efforts with the NMA through a liaison committee in order to improve the image of the medical profession and to prod Congress into enacting health legislation directed at health and medical care for all the poor and the disadvantaged. This cooperation is not mere rhetoric. An example of real achievement can be seen in the establishment of a mobile health unit in Chicago under the auspices of the Chicago Medical Society, mostly white, and a group of black doctors, the Cook County Physicians. The AMA contributed $50,000 for this endeavor. At the same time the NMA has established a fund to set up an organization which will finance comprehensive care provided by the private sector of medicine in Washington, D.C. The money will come from loans of $1,000 from each member of this organization plus a 90 per cent completed loan from the federal government.

In spite of these optimistic signs of progress, not all leaders of the NMA are enthusiastic about a marriage with the AMA and the wealthier, more powerful elements of American medicine. Some black medical leaders feel the AMA has forfeited its right to be the major voice of medicine and its problems. Certainly, it will take a long time for real trust and understanding to develop between the whites and blacks; the alienation of blacks in the American medical profession has resulted in too great a psychic scarring over a long period of time.

Since black physicians may now join white societies, the question has been raised as to the necessity of the NMA. Dr. Curtis, associate professor of psychiatry at Cornell, argues for integration of the NMA with the AMA: "The system is far too complex to be understandably analyzed, managed, or predicted on the basis of skin color or race alone. My own inclination is to hasten the day when the NMA will have no further need to exist as a separate organization of black doctors, but will be able to exert greater influence by energetic involvement in AMA organizational activities, leading the profession at large into a more responsible and more responsive role in terms of the health care of all Americans."[21]

It should be obvious, nevertheless, that the de jure progress toward full equality is not enough. The newer mood in the black community is a more militant demand through protest marches and insistent pressure by such black lay organizations as the Urban League, NAACP, and the Medical Commission for Human Rights. The NMA is needed more than ever before; it, too, has become a more activist organization. At the 1970 meeting, the NMA assessed each of its members one hundred dollars to recruit potential medical talent in high schools and academic colleges. Approximately 300 black students were expected to enter medical schools that fall, a marked increase over five years ago. The NMA has also taken on a pioneering crusade to blaze ways for the delivery of medical services to the poor and the disadvantaged. The goal is not limited to the blacks but to all people.

Likewise, there has been a significant change in the attitude and policy of the AMA during the last five years. In the past the AMA leaders spent millions of dollars employing lobbyists and advertising agencies to prevent new and progressive health legislation. This is no longer the policy of the AMA. At the convention held in San Francisco in June 1972 a new atmosphere prevailed during the debates over resolutions. Important changes have been taking place concerning the structure of the organization. For the first time in the 157-year history of the AMA, delegates and members of the Board of Trustees who were running for high offices campaigned before state and county medical societies. There was increased pressure for delegates to be elected directly by the members and for candidates to publish their platforms. There were also suggestions for new limitations on the tenure of the Board of Trustees. And the president in 1971, Dr. Wesley Hall, was challenged by high officials about changes he proposed in the structure and policies of the AMA — no president had ever been openly criticized before. The House voted to admit medical students to full membership for the first time, and the first voting delegate from the new House staff section was seated. The recognition accorded to young doctors and medical students was another sign of fundamental change. And perhaps the most important measure was a 1971 resolution, passed by the House of Delegates, to suspend any state or local societies from the AMA if they refused membership to any black doctor because of race. The overriding theme of the 1972 convention was the need for change.

The permanent shape of the AMA is yet uncertain, but now that the younger generation of doctors and students have their entrance into policy-making assured, there is hope for a more enlightened, democratic, and humane organization. It is of interest to note that Dr. C. A. Hoffman, president of AMA in 1972, began his term in office by taking an international tour of medical systems to study their methods of operation. He concentrated his tour in England to study the success of their

National Health Service (socialized medicine) and in the Soviet Union, where he found much improvement over the last fifty years. Although Dr. Hoffman feels that medicine on a principle other than fee-for-service reduces incentive among doctors, he thinks it is possible that medicine in the United States will eventually become a government operation — but not soon. Dr. Hoffman was also planning tours of rural and inner-city areas and Indian reservations in the United States to study their medical problems at first hand.[22]

Compared with the past, the position of the black M.D. has undergone much improvement: De jure, matters look very favorable. Early in the century, when blacks in small numbers began preparing for medical careers, they enrolled in badly staffed and ill equipped schools and spent their internships and residencies in small hospitals of poor quality. Rarely were they able to become accredited specialists. Today, on the other hand, there are two first-rate black medical schools, Meharry and Howard. There are openings for black medical graduates in almost every hospital in the country; application forms for admission do not require stating race. There are black specialists in every association. A few have served as presidents of local medical societies, and one has been a delegate to the AMA. A number have risen to important teaching and research positions in white medical schools. The success that black M.D.'s have achieved under incredible handicaps throughout the history of American black medicine is an outstanding example of the will to fight for full equality.

The American society must be aware of the dangers of tokenism, however, and we should realize from history that although progress has been made in a branch of treatment of blacks, neither the black doctor nor the black citizen can be expected to be satisfied fully until justice is wholly achieved. Rev. Martin Luther King was well aware of the situation when he wrote that tokenism is, in itself, not to begin a process but rather to end it — asking blacks to accept half a loaf and then to wait willingly for the other half to be distributed in crumbs over a protracted time by a hypocritical gesture is not a first constructive step. Rev. King did not think that 22 million American blacks should be expected to be grateful for the halting and inadequate attempts of our society to catch up with the basic rights the black should have automatically inherited centuries ago by virtue of his membership in the human family and his American birthright.[23] For this reason the black doctor in America cannot wait, nor can we.

MEETING THE CHALLENGE

The pivotal issue, underlying discussions of all proposals for national health programs, deals with an emerging social philosophy regarding health care. This philosophy affirms that the availability of good health care is a right, to be enjoyed by all citizens — rather than a privilege to be limited by considerations of race, religion, political belief, or economic or social conditions. . . . The development and preservation of good health requires a national commitment with well defined purposes and explicit goals.

"The Need for a New Health Care Policy in the United States,"
Interreligious Task Force on Health Care[1]

Having ventured into the diagnosis and prognosis of our medical health crisis, I would be violating the first tenet of my Hippocratic oath if I did not comment on some suggestions for the solution of this critical situation. I am not a sociologist, a medical economist, nor a medical politician speaking in behalf of the vested interests of my profession. But the time has come, and I hope not too late, for every physician in whatever specialty to meet the challenge of the health crisis and remember his oath to serve his fellow man.

More than ever before there is an awareness among the leaders of our nation of the health problem in the United States. But that awareness alone by no means assures that effective action will be taken soon. For over forty years the health of the American people has been kicked around — a political football. The small group of medical men who in the 1920's had the courage and foresight to warn Congress of the urgency for change were labelled revolutionaries and Communists by the die-hard forces who had their feet on the brakes of progress. In 1939 the first attempt at passing national compulsory health insurance was made and failed. President Truman, too, proposed such a plan in 1949, only to be thwarted by a reluctant Congress. Now everybody wants to get on the bandwagon with so-called national health insurance plans to save us from a medical catastrophe.

Labor wants national health insurance to eliminate the hassle at the bargaining table over health fringe benefits. Management wants national health insurance because health insurance premiums are a significant and rapidly rising component of overall labor costs. The medical-industrial complex think they would benefit from some form of national health insurance because their experience with Medicare and Medicaid has been profitable. For the voluntary private nonprofit hospitals, almost any program of national health insurance would be better than the present Medicaid. Commercial insurance companies are not totally opposed to national health insurance if such a program could be structured to retain the advantages of competition and the profit incentive. The American Medical Association, which has opposed any form of national health insurance for over forty years, has also offered its Medicredit plan. At the 1969 Republican governors' conference, even the most ardent states righters voted enthusiastically to support Governor Rockefeller's national health insurance proposals. Such an unprecedented coalition foreshadows the inevitability of some form of national health insurance, but what form?

Congress has found itself involved in furious debate over various national health insurance plans during the last four sessions. Since the enactment of Medicare and Medicaid, a pluralistic rash of health bills has erupted, proposed by both Republican and Democratic congressmen. These bills range from Senator Edward Kennedy's Health Security Act, a compulsory tax-supported national health insurance bill; to President Nixon's health partnership act, glamorizing the Health Maintenance Organization plans (HMO); to the AMA's Medicredit, a voluntary system of income tax credits for all Americans to offset the cost of private health insurance. In between there are a number of partial plans such as the Catastrophic Insurance program and other plans limited to providing support for research and treatment of strokes, cancer, and so on. Although these plans address themselves to the same basic issues, they differ in the amounts of benefits to be provided and in the way they should be financed and administered. Some plans, such as the Kennedy-Griffith bill, call for a major overhaul of the health care system; others would only add on to (or tinker with) the present system of delivering medical care. Dr. Edmund Casey, former president of the NMA, has said that all the plans before Congress have "addressed themselves to how we are going to pay the doctor. This is not our concern. Our concern is how we are going to deliver health care . . . to all the population, particularly the areas where there are no physicians."[2]

The 92nd Congress held hearings in which they listened to hundreds of experts and non-experts, and collected thousands of pages of information and rhetoric. Yet Congress adjourned, and no national health legislation was enacted. Meanwhile, the ghetto continues to exist as an apartheid society which we have created through neglect and discrimination. Long debates in Congress over proposals, while perhaps unavoidable, do nothing to meet the urgency of the health crisis in the inner cities.

The fact remains that no matter how many theories are advanced, no matter how much advice is offered, the health problem of poor blacks demands *immediate* action. The black ghetto resident does not need to be told what he wants from medicine; he knows. The ghetto resident does not ask for more than is his right. He wants first of all, a personal doctor who is available for him and his family. He wants what he has never had before — accessibility, availability, and continuity of medical services, and at a price he can afford. He wants a full range of services given in a setting of human dignity. He wants access and easy availability not only to medical care for emergency situations but also to preventive services such as immunization for all contagious diseases for his children. Finally, he wants access to facilities for early detection of disease for himself and his wife. Many black citizens also want a voice in the management of their own health centers. There are many intelligent, educated blacks who want and are able to participate in planning the health services in their own community — not to control the medical treatment, but to help in designing and overseeing the local health centers. The real question then is *how* to implement the necessary tools to meet these desires and needs.

In the 1960's Congress authorized several programs designed to better meet the health needs of the poor and disadvantaged, and as a pediatrician who had long been bothered by the failure of a system based on private, fee-for-service practice, I was gratified to note some of the results of these programs. One approach that has been utilized is the Regional Medical Plans (RMP's). The concept of regionalization as a means to meet health needs effectively and economically dates back several decades.[3] During the 1930's, Assistant Surgeon-General Joseph W. Mountain was one of the earliest pioneers urging this approach for the delivery of health services. The National Committee on the Costs of Medical Care also focused attention in 1932 on the potential benefits of regionalization. In that same year the Bingham Associates Fund initiated the first comprehensive regional effort to improve patient care in the United States. This program linked the hospitals and programs for continuing education of physicians in the state of Maine with the university centers of Boston. Advocates of regionalization next gained national attention more than a decade later in the report of the Commission on Hospital Care. As early as 1948, Oscar Ewing, the Administrator of Federal Security under President Truman, advocated community planning.

In 1967 the federal government awarded the first operating RMP grants. The concept of the program was that RMP's would act as a catalyst to bring agents (i.e., doctors, hospitals, consumers) together to start local projects and provide start-up money. Initially, the program was for specific disease categories — cancer, stroke, and heart disease — but the focus changed and eventually the projects ranged from providing educational and training activities to funding mobile health units. By 1973 there were 56 operating RMP's, most of them involved in delivering health services.[4] No one would argue that the program did not have its faults, but it is disturbing to note that President Nixon's budget for fiscal 1973 cuts off funding for RMP's, without replacing them with a better program.

The same is true for the OEO-funded neighborhood health centers program. This program was begun in 1966 to demonstrate new health care delivery systems. In 1972, 80 projects were in operation, serving about 2½ million persons at a cost of 108.3 million dollars. Of these projects, 25 were neighborhood health centers (24 others had been transferred previously to the Department of Health, Education, and Welfare).[5] Typically, these offered a full range of family-centered health services, with emphasis on preventive care and early treatment of disease. Other OEO projects involved restructuring hospital outpatient departments, organizing prepaid group practice plans for poor families, establishing community-wide health networks, and designing projects for rural areas. Again, no one would claim the program did not have its share of inefficiency, but an evaluation study showed that in terms of providing comprehensive and continuous care to poor families, in a setting they could accept with their dignity intact, these model programs succeeded (Interestingly, in over half of the centers studied in this evaluation, it was found that the local medical and dental societies were not involved.).

But in 1973, another form of neighborhood health centers was established under Title I of the Demonstration Cities and Metropolitan Development Act of 1966 (Model Cities). This program was designed to demonstrate how the general welfare of people living in slums and blighted areas could be substantially improved in cities of all sizes and in all parts of the country. It called for a comprehensive attack on all social, economic, and physical problems to develop new and imaginative model neighborhoods through technical and financial assistance. The Department of Housing and Urban Development (HUD) had final administrative authority for this program. A Model City Policy Group composed of representatives from the Departments of Agriculture; Commerce; Labor; Justice; and Health, Education, and Welfare and the OEO were in charge of this program. A central goal of this extensive organization was to combat disease and improve the overall living conditions for people in these areas.

In 1966 President Lyndon Johnson promised a health center in every ghetto. To prove to the nation that his promise was not mere rhetoric, he directed his black Secretary of Housing and Urban Development, Robert Weaver, to call together the representatives of the OEO, HEW, the Department of Labor, and the Bureau of Budget to set up plans to develop integrated Neighborhood Health Centers (NHC) throughout the nation. During the last 5 years, 1.2 million citizens in 115 communities in 37 states have been receiving good medical care through government subsidies which average about $183.6 million a year. NHC's are found in various locations, though most are within districts of the poor white, black, and ethnic groups. These centers serve the community in nondescript re-modelled warehouses, in shopping centers, in mountainous areas as well as in available old buildings within the heart of many a ghetto.

Now, in 1973, the Model Cities program is being termi-nated, oeo is being dismantled, and while some of the neigh-borhood health centers are being shifted to hew, there is no announced federal plan to build on or expand the successes of these programs.

Certainly, it is the task of the federal government to con-sider the overall picture presented by the programs of the 1960's. It may well be that there were waste and inefficiency and even failures, but it is incumbent on our President and leg-islators to consider, also, the individual projects that had an important impact on the communities they served. Several come to mind that I would like to discuss in some detail.

The Watts-Willowbrook health program could be said to have evolved directly as a result of the riots in that area in 1965. The area contained in 1965 approximately 70,000 persons, most of whom were black and suffering from political, social, and economic deprivation.[6] The people in this area were victims of poverty and illness; sanitation was bad, and housing dilapidated. In 1965 the ratio of physicians to patients was 1:3,000; the main source of medical care was the county hospital, which was 12 miles away and took 2 hours and $1.75 to reach. The interested residents of the area had been trying for years to secure funding for a hospital but without success. The McCone Commission, appointed to investigate the 1965 Watts riot, recommended that a new hospital be built. A combination of RMP and OEO grant money to the University of Southern California allowed for planning the needed facility. In 1967, a multipurpose health center was opened. Other grants allowed the center to continue and provided money for a 365-bed hospital and for a post-graduate medical school. While fraught with problems all along the way, Dr. Rodney Powell, the former medical director, said, "The plan is working very well; for the first time comprehensive health and medical care is available and easily accessible to all residents in that area."[7]

The Mile Square Health Center is another OEO-funded project which has been serving 25,000 blacks, one third of whom live in a Chicago high-rise housing project.[8] This district is one of the most critical pockets of poverty and has one of the poorest health records in the nation — an infant mortality rate, for example, of 46 per 1,000 live births. Among the services offered in the Mile Square program are public health nurses and community aides who work in the homes; ambulatory primary care provided by doctors, nurses, and social workers; and association with Presbyterian-St. Luke's, a teaching hospital affiliated with the University of Illinois, which provides inpatient care for those in the target area who need it.

In its first year of operation (1968) the Mile Square project registered 9,800 individuals from among the 4,000 families in the area it was to serve. Half of the families had been visited at home, and Dr. Lashof, the project director, was "struck by the number of disorders, both medical and social, as well as the number of families that can be classified as multiple problem families. . . . To measure success in such a family is difficult, but we have seen improvement and aides are continuing their contacts."[9]

Federal-community projects often meet an operational crisis; they are forced to face the fact that politics still enters into health care. A case in point is that of a community health program serving 190,000 indigent people, mostly blacks, in the impoverished Delta area of Mississippi. The Delta Health Center, located in the all-black town of Mound Bayou, Mississippi, was a pioneering outpatient facility established in 1965 by Dr. Jack Geiger of Tufts University (and run by it until 1971).[10] The project was never popular with either the Mississippi state government or the state medical society because it was publicly funded and outside their control.

Also in Mound Bayou was a small community hospital which is the main source of inpatient care for the thousands of impoverished blacks in the four counties composing the Delta area. It was falling into insolvency until rescued by an OEO grant in 1967. In the spring of 1972 OEO insisted upon and got a merger between the hospital and the health center (formerly funded and administered separately); this "corporation" is now subject to the governor's veto, a power granted for the first time by OEO.

In 1972, Governor Waller, with the firm backing of the state medical society, vetoed a $5.5 million OEO grant to the center, claiming that too much money went for administrative costs and not enough for medical care. OEO overrode the governor's veto, whereupon the state hospital commission refused to renew the hospital's license to operate. The American Public Health Association investigated the project and urged that the hospital be allowed to stay open, claiming that the hospital's faults were being corrected.

At the heart of the problem is the fact that the people served by the Delta Health Center and the hospital are almost totally dependent on it for their health services. Statistics show that while formerly "almost half the black births occurred outside of hospitals, and essentially 100 per cent of white births occurred inside hospitals," it is now the case that as many black babies are born in Mound Bayou Hospital "as in all the other white hospitals in the four counties combined." Meanwhile, the health of the Delta region patients (by now the number has reached more than 32,000) is seriously jeopardized. It remains to be seen whether or not the Delta community health–hospital project survives the political traumas inherent in state-federal liaisons.

During the last five years a revolutionary health plan, the

free clinic, has sprung up as an answer to the pervading lack of care for particular segments of our population. It is looked upon by many as a "flea on the hide of the elephantine medical system." Still, it offers some illuminating concepts, which we would do well to study. These free clinics are worth examining because of their humanitarian appeal, their idealism, and because they are the offspring of the movement for social change. The movement is founded on the convictions that the American medical system does not meet the people's needs and that it must be radically restructured. The clinics are purely local community efforts and are controlled by the people who use and work in them. In most instances they attempt to serve as an example of good health care and a model for the future. Their greatest good has come from challenging existing health services as well as providing their own.

The first of these free, or storefront, clinics opened its doors in 1967 in the Haight-Ashbury area of San Francisco.[11] In spite of initial (and in some cases continuing) opposition by the power structure, and in spite of chronic shortages of money and medical personnel, free clinics have experienced a growth that can only be described as incredible. Free clinics began in recognition of the need to treat drug-related problems, they now provide a variety of services. (One clinic in Minneapolis even offers veterinary services.) Free clinics are designed to serve the needs of a particular community, and since these needs vary greatly, so do the clinics. What they do have in common, however, is that the services they provide are available without charge and without red tape. Their sources of income are any one of or a combination of the following: federal, state, or county funds; group or individual donations; foundation grants; proceeds of fund-raising events held for individual clinics; or street solicitation (panhandling). One clinic in California derives its main financial support from the local medical society. By and large, free clinics can be classified by the population they serve; some serve particular neighborhoods (poverty or transient areas, for the most part); others provide general medical services to young people; and the third kind offers specific services, such as drug or VD treatment clinics.

Free clinics, however good they might be, are merely stop-gaps. Obviously they can provide care to only a very small part of the population in some cities where the need is greatest, but their limited role can be viewed as nothing more than a bandage applied to a sick patient — the patient being our medical system that has failed.

The Pilot City Health Center, Minneapolis

Based on my years of involvement with the health problems of the poor blacks, if I were a resident of an inner city with a family of four children, of all the plans being offered today I should prefer the kind of health and medical care which is being offered by the Pilot City Health Center (PCHC). We cannot expect Utopia overnight, but the PCHC, which is one of 60 activated units in the country at a cost of $100 million to the federal government, offers much more than the residents in that sector ever had before.[12] In an actual sense it has put into working effect "The Right to Health." It is preventing suffering and saving the lives of many men, women, and children. It is eliminating the medical apartheid; it is substituting for the "separate-and-unequal" principle that of equity and social justice.

The history of the Pilot City Health Center is a dramatic story of what started as a community "operation bootstrap." The target area includes one of the poorest sections of Minneapolis and one with the highest concentrations of blacks. Before 1966, the residents of the community had access to little or no health care. The area had one black doctor in private practice; the white doctors who preceded him had followed their patients out to the suburbs. The only medical care available was episodic and for an emergency. Private doctors outside the area were too expensive and too distant to be reached by most of the community. This area encompasses the city's highest concentration of low-income families. Many families have only one parent, many receive AFDC, a high rate of unemployment is constant, there are a large number of drug addicts, and the crime rate is high. Because of the magnitude of this urban blight, a small group of residents in 1967 formed a new community organization, Tactical Advisory Committee (TAC), in order to pull themselves up by their bootstraps.

By June 1967 the first phase of planning was completed. In July a $50,000 planning grant was allocated which enabled professionals and lay residents to set goals for the PCHC under the supervision of TAC. With the backing of Dr. C. A. Smith, health commissioner of Minneapolis, TAC surveyed the community and established the needs and priorities for health care. By September the operational plan for the Pilot City program was completed. In October 1967, TAC was superseded by an elected board called the Technical Advisory Committee Services to Implement Community Services (TACTICS). TACTICS was composed of 16 resident members and 60 agency representatives appointed by their respective agencies. The operational plan for the overall program was funded in January 1968, and the health component was approved the following June. Funding for the building facilities came from HUD ($500,000 plus another $22,000 for temporary construction work). HEW added another $100,000. The city of Minneapolis provided $320,000 in bond issue funds. Local business contributed $90,000. The Minneapolis Health Department with the approval of TACTICS signed a contract with Hennepin County General Hospital to provide jointly all medical services.

Bethel Synagogue in north Minneapolis was purchased by the city in May 1968. In October, remodeling began which included provisions for receptionist's space, privacy for interviewing, emergency care, examining rooms, nurses' stations, and laboratory and dental facilities as well as appropriate staff rooms.

The original goals were to provide family-oriented, team-based, comprehensive continuous health care for everyone in that community — goals more easily formulated than implemented. Under what seemed to be insurmountable obstacles, the PCHC began two chaotic and discouraging years of operation. It was a case of too many cooks almost spoiling the broth. Internal conflicts, widespread frustrations, lack of faith in the establishment by the residents, inadequacy of the physical plant, lack of sufficient medical and paramedical staff, insecurity over permanence of funding — all were factors tending to divide rather than to unite the lay directors of the project. To add to the turmoil, feuding between the black separationists and the integrationists caused meetings to end in one big brawl. As Dr. Donald Spigner, who became medical director in July 1971, said, "I found the Pilot City Health Center an uncoordinated octopus."

With the appointment of Dr. Spigner the PCHC took on new viability. Chaos was converted into planned order; discontent changed into trust and unity. In less than a year, Dr. Spigner's policies introduced planned techniques for the delivery of health care to all the residents and their children. By holding weekly open discussions of the entire staff, he was able to resolve the divisive influence of the black separationists and the integrationists. He published in-house letters to supervise training in basic skills of the volunteer workers. He invoked an entirely new system of outpatient department primary medical care. He reduced to a minimum the large amount of pilfering which had gone on previously. He used floodlights in front of the center to light up parking lots, and he hired a security guard to work late in the evenings. Also, he raised the standards of sanitary safety to meet the legal requirements. Dr. Spigner's dedication to PCHC and his work to acquaint the county commissioners with the needs and goals of the center soon paid dividends. Of special importance were the group unit lectures established in health education for parents of schoolchildren; intensive community education for all area residents was given high priority.

The most difficult of all obstacles was the financial one. When Dr. Spigner first arrived, the center was kept from going under by four different federal agencies. The U.S. Public Health Service, an absentee landlord, was not really actively concerned but had some fiscal responsibility. The local Social Service Administration offered services provided by HEW through the Social Security Act. The County Welfare Family Planning limited its funds to those on county relief. It became imperative to unify the funding derived from the several agencies not actually involved in active participation. That the medical director was successful in the delicate area of personal relationships as well as in the vast area of the complex mechanics of the program is a testimony to his great insight and applied talent.

By the end of 1970, Pilot City Health Center had about 14,000 clients and saw an average of 150 patients per day, at least half of whom were served on a walk-in basis. The services provided by PCHC are numerous and deserve to be examined more closely.

Dental Care. In order to meet the urgent needs of the community, especially for the children, a dental department was planned and implemented with five part-time dentists. Over half of the children under 16 years of age had never had a dental examination. The department quickly developed a waiting list and is caring for a large number of patients who sought only dental care at the center. By the end of the fiscal year 1970 the dental department was faced with the problem of more demand than supply. As we go into 1973 there is still a long waiting list for dental services.

Ambulatory Services. One of the most important reasons for the previous underutilization of medical facilities was the lack of an ambulance service. This has been a high priority on Dr. Spigner's list of concerns. For any patient or child who cannot get to the clinic by any other means, a 10-hour emergency ambulance service to the county general hospital or the PCHC is now in use. This service has at its disposal a fully equipped ambulance, a bus with emergency equipment, and a station wagon. The drivers are well trained in first aid.

X Ray and Laboratory. An X-ray department and laboratory were installed in crowded and inadequate space, but by the end of fiscal 1971 the laboratory staff had grown to five full-time technologists who were doing over 7,000 tests a month. The X-ray department occupied two fully outfitted rooms with a staff of four X-ray technicians and two aides.

Pharmacy. This department was manned by three pharmacists and a pharmacy intern. The goal is to provide patients with rapid service and time to counsel patients on their prescribed medications.

Speech Therapy. In 1968 the Minnesota Easter Seals Association hired a full-time speech therapist for the center. She surveyed the schools and identified 270 children needing therapy, 91 of whom were in need of emergency help. Although there were no facilities for audiology, the therapist rendered valuable help to 58 of these children.

Mental Health Services. Because of the large number of adults, teenagers, and children with behavioral and mental disturbances who had never been screened by professionals, the first goal in this most neglected field was to count and to evaluate patients in need of treatment. It was first necessary to persuade the patient to seek mental health services and to follow through when referred. In the six-month period from July to December 1970, an average of 25 per cent of referrals were classified as self-referrals, consisting of individuals and families who were "hurting." The family counselors and social workers were especially helpful in making sure that these clients kept their appointments. They also gave the patients an empathy they had never known before.

The first hurdle to overcome in the mental health program was financial. In the original grant, funds were deleted for mental health services. Fortunately, the state of Minnesota, through the Hennepin County Mental Health Board, gave a grant of $55,000 which was to be matched by the National Institute of Mental Health.

A clinical psychologist, several psychiatric social workers, and several volunteer health workers began a program of crisis intervention, long-term treatment, group work, and psychological screening. The addition of these persons has made possible the development of group programs which have been highly successful as of this writing. A consulting psychiatrist on a one-tenth basis was also secured. By January 1971, 325 children aged 2 to 16 years and their families had been given counselling and treatment for all types of mental and emotional disturbances. This had been accompanied by marital, family, and group discussions of personal problems.

The focus of the mental health program is upon working with families, especially those in crisis. In order to do this, the staff often has treatment sessions in the home. This provides an added opportunity for observation and interaction with the family members. It is also a convenience for the family to be seen at home rather than in the center. This naturalistic setting is more comfortable and less artificial than the usual office visit. It also maximizes the possibility of including the father in therapy, whereas the office visit often omits the father. Sometimes the very need to organize the family for the visit of the therapist is the occasion for one of the few times that the family actually acts as a cohesive organization.

Treatment services for children frequently are in the context of family therapy. However, some individual visits are held at the health center. When indicated, children may be seen at school, and visits with some adolescents occur in the street or at a local lunch counter. Children have available individual assessment for a broad range of behavioral, learning, and intrapersonal problems. An integral part is to assure referral for dysfunctional problems such as learning disabilities. This is facilitated by the close working relationship between the mental health and the pediatric staff. Clinical nursing specialists in pediatrics have received general training in screening for developmental problems. The mental health staff is involved in further specific training so that eventually all preschool children will receive screening for early identification and remediation.

Some 13.1 per cent of the students at the schools in the Pilot City area are from minority groups. Of all the 69 elementary schools in Minneapolis, the 3 in the Pilot City area were ranked by school administrators as the most difficult to manage. Of the 17 junior high schools the one in this district was ranked first in number of dropouts. Since the children of all ages attending schools in the Pilot City are in a high risk group for school failure, it is clear that a mental health program is a must. Services to youth (adolescents and young adults) are being developed to provide something more than the traditional services. The staff at North High School feel overwhelmed with the problems of apathetic youth who are leaving school severely handicapped for obtaining employment with their limited academic skills. Development of services to meet the needs of school dropouts and young adults is ongoing and quite probably will include a storefront, drop-in counselling service open in the evening. It is also possible that drug use programs may be included in this format.

The total mental health services are an integral part of PCHC. They are easily accessible to the entire population of Pilot City. They are flexible in matching appropriate service with specific needs. The neighborly concern of informally trained men and women, blacks and whites, can often dispel the anxiety and mistrust associated with more formal approaches. Although the volunteers share in a large part of the program, direct treatment is entirely in the hands of psychologists and psychiatrists.

Nutrition. A nutritionist was hired early in the program to deal with problems of PCHC clients — limited budgets, inaccessible food markets, and so forth. Still the sole member of the department (because limited funds prohibit expansion), she consults with many day care centers in the area, schools, and the health center staff, and also provides direct service to patients.

Public Health Nursing. Several nurses have worked with the clinic on assignment from the Minneapolis Health Department, but, by and large, this remains a referred service.

Drugs. A methadone treatment program was initiated in 1969 and swelled rapidly. The experience of this component of PCHC is illustrative of the problems and possibilities of a neighborhood health center:

Initially, the goals were to assist the addicts to change their life styles through group work and job and educational opportunities with methadone as a stepping stone. The social worker became engulfed in the program, as did the internist and, of necessity, the pharmacy.

A subtle struggle for leadership ensued as the internist began admitting people to the program unilaterally. (All candidates were to be screened by a committee of staff and addicts, but the committee met only weekly.) The number of participants swelled and not all of them were involved in groups.

The idea of establishing a community education program utilizing the addicts to speak to various groups came early. However, the ability to take in money and pay honorariums to these individuals was not within reach of the center at the time. The social worker developed a private foundation for this purpose and focused on these goals.

Thus, the methadone program could be seen as taking several directions: a group involved in education and socialization, and groups receiving primarily medical treatment (maintenance and supposed detoxification), without unified leaderships and program goals.

Meanwhile, the community aides were still trying to carry out the original goals of the social service section.[13]

Glenwood Clinic

The Glenwood Clinic is a satellite outpatient department of the PCHC, about two miles from the center. It is an offspring of the original prenatal baby clinic under the Minneapolis City Board of Health. When I took over the weekly clinic in 1967, we moved into a three-room unit, truly a storefront house of medicine, limited to the care of well and sick children.

Every Wednesday a public health nurse, two aides, and I set up shop. We were assisted by another aide who has lived in the Glenwood area and knows most of the patients. During the week this aide is available to receive calls and acts as a liaison between the patients and the clinic. She also makes calls on Fridays to read Mantoux tests and gives reports on throat cultures. Wednesday is well utilized by anyone who wants to register. If they can afford it, patients pay a small fee for the services; all others receive services, including medicines, free.

There are no oriental rugs, no oil paintings in our clinic; the facility is rented from the Minneapolis Housing Authority for one dollar a year. The first floor has a kitchen and a big living room which serves as a receiving office. There are snacks and coffee in the kitchen along with a playpen and toys and several borrowed folding chairs. A desk for registration and an old folding table with an ancient scale on it are off to one side, out of the reach of the runabouts. The two nursing aides act as hostesses, and welcome is expressed in their faces. After the patients are registered, they walk or are carried to an upstairs room over which I preside before an old table with the few necessary things to fulfill my role as an emeritus pediatrician. The immunizations and other sundry tasks are done by one of the nursing aides; there is always a drawer filled with suckers.

This clinic resembles the outpatient clinics in primitive countries. With one pediatrician, an excellent public health nurse, two nurses aides, a local voluntary counselor, and an ambulance to see that the patients without transportation can keep their appointments, we hold our heads high and claim 100 per cent immunizations and no known contagious diseases for which there are specifics. We have full cooperation from our parent PCHC and other allied health agencies. We go to bed each night feeling "We are our brother's keeper."

The value of having a clinic such as Pilot City, offering as many services as it does, can perhaps be best demonstrated by citing several cases of exemplary importance. In the first instance, a family with five children moved to Minnesota from Arkansas in December 1969. Previous medical care had been sporadic; the family had obtained medicines for illnesses only when they had been able to afford them. Immunizations had also been given sporadically. After moving to Minneapolis, the family came to the Pilot City Health Center for treatment of acute illness. Physical exams were given to each child. Six-year-old Joyce had extremely poor teeth, and care was initiated for her in the dental clinic. Richard, age five, Douglas, age two, and Marie, age ten months, all had heart murmurs. At least one of these was due to an organic defect and may require heart surgery. Complete immunizations and periodic visits, which include counseling on diet and hygiene, are being carried out for all the children.

A second case concerns a ten-year-old boy, Kevin, who came to the clinic for a physical examination; he had had immunizations at various health centers but no physical exam. It was noted that he was of short stature, had extremely poor dentition and very dry skin. When a detailed history was obtained, his mother mentioned that he had had convulsions in the neonatal period. A serum calcium was tested and a diagnosis of hypocalcemia was made. Kevin was immediately referred to the University of Minnesota for further testing and treatment.

A final example is the case of George, a six-year-old boy who was brought in by his mother for a routine physical exam; a schoolteacher had requested the exam because of the child's hyperactivity and short attention span in class. It was discovered that George had a history of many ear infections; they had been treated by the county general hospital and various private doctors. Physicals and immunizations had been given at well-child clinics. The hearing tests previously administered had been recorded as "unsuccessful." The physical exam at PCHC revealed scarring of both eardrums, and an audiogram revealed marked hearing loss in the right ear and moderate loss in the left. The child was scheduled for ear-nose-throat consultation in the clinic, and then admitted to the hospital for polyethylene tubes and the removal of his tonsils and adenoids. Moderate improvement in hearing occurred, and a hearing aid was provided. The child's progress in school improved markedly.

These three cases illustrate the seriousness of scattered and incomplete treatment as well as the possibilities of tragic consequences for those seriously ill, impoverished children who do not receive medical care when it is urgently needed. These cases, alone, testify to the necessity of professionally staffed clinics which should exist in every neighborhood, open to all those in need of treatment.

The poor blacks in this community, served by the Pilot City program, have for the first time had access to the mainstream of medicine on an equal basis. They now have a personal physician who is available to the family twenty-four hours a day. Pregnant mothers no longer are chiefly delivered by granny midwives with no formal training; today all the mothers from these districts are hospitalized in either general or voluntary obstetrical wards. These are the people who once waited long hours on hard benches in charity clinics in order to obtain some medical care. They are now treated as human beings in need of medical help and not as numbers; they now have a full range of services given in a setting of dignity with a voice in the management of their own house of health.

Someday, I hope not in the too distant future, Americans will demand and get a prepaid national health insurance system which will make available to the poor and disadvantaged to whom this book is dedicated the highest quality of total health. But until the enactment of a compulsory total health plan, the programs I mentioned above deserve continued funding. I cannot view the cutoff of federal funds for these programs as anything but a step backward from the few advances that had been made in the 1960's. Our continued piecemeal tinkering with a system which has clearly outlived its usefulness is futile. Only by reforming the system itself can we expect the kind of medical sociology which will give all the people and especially the poor and the disadvantaged their inherent rights. Instead of a bandage and aspirin, what we need is radical surgery. While I am not by nature a pessimist, I find it discouraging that no comprehensive reforms seem imminent.

It seems clear that some type of legislation will be enacted and implemented similar to the Health Maintenance Organizations (HMO's). These are prepaid medical plans, wherein the participant pays a fixed fee per year in return for full medical care. The concept is not new, though it has come a long way in acceptability among the medical profession. In the 1950's when Group Health, a prepaid plan in St. Paul to which I belong, was being organized, we doctors who were interested in working in such a setting had to meet in dark corners of out of the way places to discuss it. At that time, participating in a prepaid group practice could mean expulsion from the local medical society — a threatened penalty that was ended by the courts.

The advantages of organizing medical care around HMO's are many, but the way they are organized contain pitfalls. The best plans operating today are controlled by nonprofit corporations, but it is likely that new plans will be set up on a profit-making basis, and that, I believe, would not be in the best interests of the consumers. Dr. Maurice Visscher, chairman of the Group Health Plan of St. Paul, has cogently set forth the dangers:

> It is known that the administrative expenses and profit on health insurance sold by private insurance companies in the U.S. eat up as much as half of the insurance premiums. Even more disadvantageous to the consuming public, however, is the fact that in an HMO run for profit there would be the danger that needed services would not be provided in order to increase the margin of profit. It would be very dangerous to set up a system of medical care in which private profit could be increased by depriving patients of optimal services simply to increase the profits of an insurance company or even of a corporation organized by doctors. Most physicians are deeply interested in their patient's welfare, but there are some in the medical profession as well as in other professions who are not to be trusted to put their patients' or clients' welfare ahead of their own economic advantage. In life and death matters it is not safe for the public to allow anyone to gain financial advantage out of doing less for patients than would be medically desirable.
> Ideally, HMO's should be consumer-controlled, but as an absolute minimum they must be managed on a nonprofit basis.[14]

Whatever plan is adopted by Congress should, in my opinion, include these five major principles which have been set forth by the Health Professionals for Political Action:[15]

1. Access to comprehensive health care is a right which must be assured to all citizens.
2. A financing scheme must be provided which guarantees health care regardless of a person's ability to pay. Coinsurance and deductibles in an insurance plan discriminate against the poor.
3. Any national solution to the health crisis must compel a reorganization of the health care delivery system. Thus, the federal government should set standards for personnel, facilities, and quality of care and raise the revenues for financing the national health insurance system.
4. Thoroughly comprehensive benefits must be provided, so that all the health care needs of the patient are met.
5. Aggressive action must be taken by the government to get health care to inner cities and rural areas.

Some may consider these points radical, yet radical steps are needed to eliminate the dual system of medicine that has existed in this country for too long. There are no immediate solutions that will create a medical Utopia overnight, but some of the programs the government has funded in the 1960's have provided partial answers for the medically disenfranchised, and we must, I feel, go forward from there. In the last analysis, solutions to the medical crisis will be reached only by a total commitment of doctors, consumers, and legislators to provide adequate and reasonably priced — if necessary, free — medical care for all the citizens of our country.

SUMMING UP

We have the knowledge, wealth and ability in America to assure
that every American gets the health care he needs and is not faced
by financial ruin in the process. We can guarantee each other
good health care. The question is, do we have the will to do it?

Edward M. Kennedy, *In Critical Condition*
(New York: Simon and Schuster, 1972), p. 18

American medicine has long been a principal victim of our nation's inverted sense of values. The scientific triumphs of
American medicine include the discovery of miracle drugs, the
transplantation of organs, and the discovery of new and powerful vaccines, but the portion of the population denied the
benefits of these advances consists of many millions. We have
allowed military needs to rank far above human needs. The
affluent have access to the highest quality of medical care and
they know how to get it. The poor and deprived usually get
only the crumbs of medical care or none at all.

It is primarily the blacks to whom I have directed my concern in this book. How far have we come and how much further must we go to eliminate once and for all this terrible
disease of racism which has sickened our society? In my research on these questions I have tried to portray an accurate
picture, using the most recent data as they relate to the general health crisis of the black population, the tragedy of this
health crisis specifically among black children, the prejudice

that has long thwarted the ambitions of black medical students, the struggle of black doctors to achieve equal status with white doctors, and finally, the seeds of meeting the challenge that have sprouted and how they can be nurtured to bear fruit.

The Black Health Crisis. Racism and poverty are two sides of the same coin, and the black population has felt the full impact of both. These two elements of American society are inseparable from the black health crisis: an attack on the problems of health must include an all-out effort to eradicate racism and poverty. Our present system of private fee-for-service medical care leaves out large numbers of blacks. This accounts for the higher morbidity and mortality rates, for the greater incidence of illnesses, and for the lack of preventive health knowledge among the blacks, as well as among the poor of all colors, in all sections of the country.

Since 1900 there has been a dramatic improvement in the overall picture of the health of black people, but a large gap between white and black health statistics still remains owing to the double standard in the primary delivery of medical services.

In 1964 the passage of the Civil Rights Act gave blacks the necessary means of fighting discrimination de jure. Title VI of this Act, which removed the separate-but-equal clause from the Hill-Burton Act (a federal measure to help finance the building and improvement of hospitals) was a specific tool for activists to use against overt discrimination. It was of essential importance, particularly in the South, where many blacks had been denied entrance to hospitals and other medical facilities for years. Unfortunately, attitudes are not easily changed by law. De facto discrimination still exists overtly in the South and covertly throughout the entire United States. The Civil Rights Commission issued a report in 1966 which revealed a failure of the enforcement of the Civil Rights Act, Title VI, in many medical facilities throughout the South; it is evident even today that illegal medical practices in regard to the blacks continue. A greater effort must be launched to combat this situation and without sufficient financing the opposition cannot be overcome.

Both overt and covert discrimination have had a devastating effect on the attitudes of the blacks toward seeking medical help. Already trapped within the poverty cycle, they receive inadequate medical care not only because of racial discrimination but because of the attitudes of white professionals toward low-income groups. They are accused of not caring about the health of their children or their own health, when the facts show that they often simply cannot afford to pay for the services. The Horatio Alger myth has no place within our present economic system. It is very difficult to get out of the clutches of poverty and pull oneself up by one's own bootstraps; as one family member said, "There are no bootstraps, there are not even any boots."

Masses of people, with the blacks among those in the forefront, have taken up the challenge to better their way of life. Progress has been made, but much remains to be done. We cannot expect blacks to close the remaining gap alone. A national effort must be made to attack the health crisis on all fronts — and the essential factors of poverty and discrimination cannot be ignored — in order to ensure the right to health for every citizen of the United States.

Health of the Black Child. The maternal and infant mortality rates of this country are a disgrace not only as a black-white comparison, but as a comparison between our national statistics and those of other Western countries, which rank far better than we do. Our children, from all races and economic levels, are a precious resource, so we say. Yet too many black children continue to grow up in the same environment of poverty and discrimination that crippled their parents. Frequently, their poor health jeopardizes their learning ability, and so the cycle will continue. These children suffer from the covert prejudicial attitudes on the part of many teachers. The physically ill or mentally disturbed black child is often ignored and receives no medical attention until his illness has reached tragic proportions.

Head Start, a federally funded national program, has begun to combat the social, psychological, and physical problems of low-income children in the United States. My own involvement with the Head Start program in Minneapolis has renewed my faith that the health crisis of black children can be remedied. But as is the case with all such national programs, the uncertainty of financial commitment is a constant threat to continuing success. We must not slacken the efforts already being made; we must insist that the health of children of all races receive top consideration within a national health plan.

The Black Medical Student. The victims of racism within our medical system have not been limited to the patients. Discrimination and poverty have also had a disastrous effect on the opportunities for black medical students. For years blacks could not even consider a career in medicine because of the attitudes of predominantly white medical schools who barred their entry by both overt and covert means. As in the case of hospital facilities, the 1964 Civil Rights Act helped to open up medical schools to the blacks. But again, de jure achievement did not, and still does not today, mean de facto success. A form of racial bias still exists concerning entrance into medical schools for the black student, the Medical College Admission Tests. There is an ongoing controversy over the use of these tests for all minority groups, whose members are screened on the same basis as the middle- and upper-middle–class white student who has usually had a far better elementary and secondary education. The long-range solution must be in the overall improvement of education for blacks at all levels of training.

Even if the bars of discrimination are removed from the medical school system, the economic problem remains. The cost of an education in preparation for a medical career today is out of reach for many white students. For the black student from a low-income family, entrance into the medical profession is a financial impossibility without scholarships and other outside assistance. The NMA has been in the forefront of the struggle to gain both entrance and financial assistance for the black student in pursuit of a career in medicine.

It is encouraging to report that over the past twenty years the number of black medical students has almost doubled; white medical schools have increased their black enrollment about fivefold in this period, and four times as many white medical schools are now open to blacks. However, as of 1972, blacks are still underrepresented in the medical profession in terms of their proportion to the general population, in terms of their interest in pursuing medical careers, and in terms of the need among blacks for medical services. Although blacks constituted 11.2 per cent of the total population in 1969, only 2.2 per cent of the physicians, less than 2 per cent of the dentists, and less than 5 per cent of the nurses in this country were black. The NMA has set a goal for a black enrollment of 12 per cent by 1975; this goal includes the aim of 12 per cent black medical graduates — in other words, the hope is to produce fully prepared doctors who have completed training, not just gained admittance to the medical program.

The Black Doctor. Once the black student has completed training and has achieved the status of doctor, ready to begin practice, the struggle is by no means over. For more than a century the black doctor has received unfair treatment from the AMA and its component societies. Hospital staff privileges, entrance into white medical societies, board certification, as well as geographical distribution of practices, all add up to reveal that the power of the AMA has kept the black physician out of the mainstream of the American medical profession for over one hundred years. The 1960's were an era of civil rights battles; there were years of painful legal action, sped up by militant protests and constant demands for de jure equality for black doctors. The hospitals of the South, closed so long to the blacks, were forced to open up to the black doctors in 1964 after the Civil Rights Act was passed and the Supreme Court struck down the separate-but-equal clause of the Hill-Burton Act.

In the 1970's, the need remains to combat not only the residue of de jure problems for the black doctor but also the de facto elements of discrimination within the American medical system. The black doctor demands full equality with the white; he has finally gained entrance into the white societies, but he still feels he is far from having total acceptance, both socially and professionally.

The new militancy of black doctors in the NMA has helped to push the AMA toward progressive change. The last several years have shown that both organizations are willing to unite efforts in certain areas in order to meet the crisis of the American medical scene. The black doctor, who has often suffered the effects of discrimination and poverty along with his black patients, is now finding some understanding among his white colleagues. I believe that the AMA, the voice of the medical profession, finally after forty years of a cold war with the government and progressive forces, is changing from a negative to a positive social force. It is still given far more to rhetoric than to action, but compared with its former attitudes the AMA has exhibited revolutionary changes. The conditions under which the black doctor can now practice have improved considerably since the AMA developed its new conscience. The

NMA continues to exert itself in the direction of profound change.

One thing is clear; blacks are no longer satisfied with tokenism and gradualism. Black doctors insist on genuine representation in, and responsibility for, the decision-making policies of white medical societies, hospitals, and medical schools. They demand an active role in the planning and servicing of medical centers. At the same time, most black professionals do not feel that the responsibility of meeting the health crisis among the underprivileged should be theirs alone. They want to join with their white colleagues in combating the national health crisis; they want whites and blacks to work together to eradicate disease among all white and black patients and raise the health standards of this country to a level which reflects equal care for all.

Meeting the Challenge. The 92nd Congress, known as an outstanding health session because of the large number of health bills passed, adopted no new major health legislation which would benefit or improve the chances for the poor blacks to get better health facilities and services. Practically all the bills passed were fringe health bills; no bill was passed that would directly combat the high morbidity and mortality rates of the black population.

The most recent, more innovative, insurance and health bills are still delayed. Meanwhile, the health problem assumes critical proportions. State and local programs have struggled on in the face of delays for a comprehensive national health plan which could meet the challenge of the crisis head on.

Since the Johnson administration, many federally funded programs have continued operating across the country. But in 1973 many of them are facing termination. My own experiences as a pediatrician with the Pilot City Health Center of Minneapolis have given me first-hand proof of the effectiveness of such programs. On a local level we have managed to provide comprehensive health services for the formerly deprived inner-city black poor. There are similar projects all over the country with many different financial sources, types of services, and political philosophies. The underlying purpose of all of them, however, is to function as stopgap measures in the serious medical crisis that exists among the blacks and all other poor families. The free clinics that have sprung up in the last few years embrace those who either mistrust or cannot afford the medical services offered on a private fee-for-service basis. These clinics are sometimes totally dependent upon voluntary help from maverick doctors who are simultaneously practicing within the medical establishment.

In conclusion, I think the case is clear: medical care equality for all is not only an urgent national need but a moral necessity. The choices this nation makes in the allocation of its resources reflect our system of values. We are indicating our priorities through this allocation, and thus far we have a far from acceptable record in total national health achievements. The mortality, morbidity, and general health statistics of the poverty-stricken, minority groups of our country give evidence of this failure. As Franklin Roosevelt said in 1933, "The test of a nation's progress is not to make the rich richer, not to add to the abundance of those who have much, but rather to provide enough to those who have too little."

I have tried in this book to make a diagnosis of the developments and trends which reveal that the health system in the United States is indeed in a state of crisis. If the problems which have been described are to be resolved, the present health system will have to undergo drastic changes. We urgently need to reshape our institutions for the provision of medical care into a concrete nationally planned system responsive to the needs of modern society and the potential of modern medical science. We need an AMA that will aggressively move forward with the NMA and bring to fruition the seeds of progressive change. We need a socially aware Congress fighting for national health legislation that is truly effective. We need medical, social, and political leaders on all levels to dedicate themselves to the priority of the right to health for all Americans. It is late in the day, but it is not *too* late to take the right road to preserve our richest resource — the health and lives of our people. An old proverb says, "He who has health has hope, and he who has hope has everything."

Notes

NOTES

The Right to Health

1. (Nashville, Tenn.: Aurora, 1970), p. 39.
2. See Milton Roemer, *The Organization of Medical Care under Social Security* (Geneva: International Labour Office, 1969), p. 7.
3. Franklin Delano Roosevelt, "An Economic Bill of Rights," in Henry Steele Commager, ed., *Documents of American History*, vol. 2 (New York: Appleton, 1963), pp. 484, 485.
4. *Wall Street Journal*, March 27, 1972, p. 8.
5. *Ibid.*
6. Schorr, *Don't Get Sick in America*, p. 136.
7. Roul Tunley, *The American Health Scandal* (New York: Harper, 1966), p. 192.
8. *Ibid.*, p. 164.
9. John C. Norman, ed., *Medicine in the Ghetto* (New York: Appleton, 1969), p. 302.
10. *Ibid.*, p. 311.
11. Richard M. Nixon, Inaugural Address, January 20, 1969.

The Black Health Crisis:
Poverty and Discrimination

1. Public Affairs Pamphlet No. 435 (New York: Public Affairs Committee, 1970), pp. 7, 8.
2. "Age Patterns in Medical Care, Illness, and Disability: United States, 1968–1969," DHEW Publication No. (HSM) 72-1026 (Rockville, Md., April 1972), 88 pp.
3. U.S. Bureau of the Census, *Statistical Abstract of the United States: 1972* (93rd ed.) (Washington, D.C., 1972).
4. New York *Times*, December 13, 1971.
5. "Infant Mortality Rates: Socioeconomic Factors," DHEW Publication No. (HSM) 72-1045 (Rockville, Md., March 1972), p. 35.
6. *Ibid.*, p. 36.
7. *Medical Tribune*, February 7, 1973, p. 15.
8. In Herbert M. Morais, *The History of the Negro in Medicine* (New York: Publishers Company, 1967), p. 6.
9. *Health Care in America*, Hearings before the Senate Subcommittee on Executive Reorganization, pt. 1, 90th Congress, 2nd sess. (Washington, D.C.: GPO, 1969), p. 462.

10. *Ibid.*, p. 470.
11. Barbara and John Ehrenreich, *The American Health Empire: Power, Profits, and Politics* (New York: Random House, 1971), p. 4.
12. John C. Norman, ed., *Medicine in the Ghetto* (New York: Appleton, 1969), p. 66.
13. Most of the information in the following paragraphs is from Max Seham, "Discrimination against Negroes in Hospitals," *New England Journal of Medicine*, vol. 27 (October 29, 1965), pp. 940ff.
14. U.S. Commission on Civil Rights, *HEW and Title VI*, U.S. Commission on Civil Rights Publication No. 22 (1970), p. 1.
15. See R. H. Ehert, "Discrimination in Hospitals: A Prescription," *Atlantic*, vol. 217 (May 1966), p. 49.
16. U.S. Commission on Civil Rights, *HEW and Title VI*.
17. *Ibid.*
18. Robert Coles, "The Doctor and Newcomers to the Ghetto," in *The American Scholar*, vol. 40 (Winter 1970–1971), pp. 72–73.
19. Anselm Strauss, "Medical Organization, Medical Care, and Lower Income Groups," mimeographed.

Health of the Black Child

1. (New York: Appleton, 1972), p. 2. Quoted here by permission of the copyright holder, the Meredith Corporation.
2. U.S. Bureau of the Census, *Statistical Abstract of the United States: 1972* (93rd ed.) (Washington, D.C., 1972), p. 329.
3. *Ibid.*, p. 55.
4. *Ibid.*, p. 57.
5. *Vital Statistics of the United States: 1967. Vol. 1: Natality* (Washington: GPO, 1969), pp. 1–21.
6. Alonzo S. Yerby, "The Disadvantaged and Health Care," *American Journal of Public Health*, vol. 56 (1966), pp. 5–9.
7. *Ibid.*, p. 8.
8. *Vital Statistics: Natality*, pp. 1–26.
9. National Center for Health Statistics, ser. 11, no. 104 (September 1970), pp. 5–6.
10. *Vital Statistics: Natality*, pp. 1–21.
11. *Vital Statistics of the United States: 1967. Vol. 2: Mortality* (Washington: GPO, 1969), pp. 3–8.
12. Personal communication, Dr. S. Rosenfeld, Minnesota State Board of Health.
13. Personal communication, Dr. Arthur J. Lesser, Maternal and Child Health Service, Department of Health, Education, and Welfare.
14. John C. Norman, ed., *Medicine in the Ghetto* (New York: Appleton, 1969), p. 88.
15. "Infant Mortality Associated with Family Socioeconomics," *Medical Tribune*, October 15, 1972, p. 6.
16. *Pediatric News*, vol. 6, p. 53.
17. *Time*, July 10, 1972, p. 64.
18. Metropolitan Life, *Statistical Bulletin*, vol. 51 (1970), p. 2.
19. Hubert Humphrey, *War on Poverty* (New York: McGraw-Hill, 1964).
20. Bullough, *Poverty, Ethnic Identity, and Health Care*, pp. 118–119.

21. Robert Coles, testimony before Senate Committee on Labor and Public Welfare, June 15, 1967.
22. Testimony before Senate Subcommittee on Nutrition, February 1969.
23. Coles, testimony, June 15, 1967.
24. Project Head Start: Health Services (Washington: OEO, n.d.), p. 5.
25. Dr. Ralph Wedgewood in a statement before the Senate Committee on Ways and Means, March 16, 1967.
26. Ibid.
27. Head Start: A Child Development Program (Washington: Office of Child Development, HEW, n.d.), p. 9.
28. Personal communication, Dr. H. J. Geiger.
29. Personal communication, Dr. Charles Pryles.
30. Personal communication, Dr. Rodney Powell.
31. Evelyn Hartman, "Head Start," Journal of School Health, vol. 37 (1967), p. 232.

The Black Student in Medicine

1. Vol. 281 (1969), p. 1274.
2. American Medical News, December 6, 1971.
3. Leonard W. Johnson, Jr., "History of the Education of Negro Physicians," Journal of Medical Education, vol. 42 (1967), p. 441; George E. Schwarz and Montague S. Lawrence, "Selected Characteristics of the Members of the National Medical Association: Preliminary Findings," Journal of the National Medical Association, vol. 62 (1970), p. 6.
4. Johnson, pp. 440–441.
5. Anne E. Crowley and Hayden C. Nicholson, "Negro Enrollment in Medical Schools," Journal of the American Medical Association, vol. 210 (1969), p. 96.
6. Ruth M. Raup and Elizabeth A. Williams, "Negro Students in Medical Schools in the United States," Journal of Medical Education, vol. 39 (1964), pp. 444–445.
7. Johnson, p. 442.
8. Dietrich Reitzes, Negroes in Medicine (Cambridge, Mass.: Harvard University Press, 1958).
9. Raup and Williams, p. 445.
10. Ibid., p. 449; Crowley and Nicholson, p. 97, table 1.
11. Crowley and Nicholson, pp. 96 and 97, table 1.
12. 1973–1974 Medical School Admission Requirements (Washington: Association of American Medical Colleges, 1972), p. 17.
13. Ibid.
14. John Z. Bowers, Lee Cogan, and E. Lowell Becker, "Negroes for Medicine: Report of a Conference," Journal of the American Medical Association, vol. 202 (1967), p. 141.
15. Crowley and Nicholson, p. 99.
16. Philip Lee, "Status of the Black Medical Student," American Medical News, April 21, 1969.
17. George Smith, paper read at MACY conference in Atlanta, February 25–27, 1968.
18. David G. Johnson, "Interpreting Medical College Admission Test Scores," paper read at MACY conference in Atlanta, February 25–27, 1968.

19. M. Alfred Haynes, "Problems Facing the Negro in Medicine Today," *Journal of the American Medical Association*, vol. 209 (1969), p. 1067.
20. Bowers et al., p. 141.
21. Crowley and Nicholson, p. 99.
22. Lloyd Elam, paper read at MACY conference in Atlanta, February 25–27, 1968.
23. James L. Curtis, *Blacks, Medical Schools, and Society* (Ann Arbor: University of Michigan Press, 1971), p. 108.
24. Bowers et al., p. 141; Joseph L. Henry, "The Problems Facing Negroes in Dental Education," *Journal of the American College of Dentists*, vol. 36 (1969), p. 238.
25. Bowers et al., p. 142.
26. Raup and Williams, p. 449.
27. Crowley and Nicholson, p. 100.
28. Haynes, pp. 11–12.
29. *American Medical News*, August 28, 1972, p. 1.
30. *Ibid.*, p. 8.
31. Haynes, p. 1068.
32. Norman, "Possible Problems," p. 164.
33. Johnson, p. 443.
34. W. M. Cobb, "A New Dawn in Medicine," *Ebony Magazine*, vol. 18 (1963), pp. 166–171.
35. Ronald Gregg, "Black Interns and Residents," *Public Health Economics*, vol. 25 (1968), p. 853.
36. Haynes, p. 1068.
37. *Ibid.*, p. 1069.
38. Herbert M. Morais, *The History of the Negro in Medicine* (New York: Publishers Company, 1968), pp. 100–101.
39. M. Elizabeth Carnegie, "Are Negro Schools of Nursing Needed Today?" *Nursing Outlook*, vol. 12 (1964), p. 55.
40. *Ibid.*, p. 52.
41. Barbara L. Tate and M. Elizabeth Carnegie, "Negro Admissions, Enrollments, and Graduations — 1963," *Nursing Outlook*, vol. 13 (1965), p. 61.
42. *Ibid.*, p. 63.
43. Mabel Keaton Staupers, "The Black Nurse and Nursing Goals," *Journal of National Medical Association*, vol. 62 (1970), p. 304.
44. Arnold C. Bellinger and Virginia S. Cleland, "A Comparative Analysis of Negro and Caucasian Nurses on Selected Organismic and Job-Related Variables," *Nursing Research*, vol. 18 (1969), pp. 534, 537.
45. Council on Dental Education, "Development of Programs to Increase Educational Opportunities for Disadvantaged Students in the Health Professions," *Journal of the American Dental Association*, vol. 80 (1970), pp. 1060, 1061.
46. *Ibid.*, p. 1060.
47. *Ibid.*, pp. 1061–1062.
48. Henry, pp. 237–238.
49. *Ibid.*, p. 238.
50. *New York Times*, April 8, 1973, News of the Week in Review, p. 6.
51. *Statistical Abstract of the United States: 1971* (Washington: GPO, 1972), p. 316.
52. Sell A. Dixon, letter to the editor, *Journal of the American Dental Association*, vol. 76 (1968), pp. 233–234.

53. Haynes, p. 1068.
54. Curtis, *Blacks, Medical Schools, and Society*, p. 162.
55. However, in the past Howard and Meharry have been the only schools who have considered how blacks will be trained to serve lower income groups or anyone else. Knowing that graduates of these two schools have served blacks in the past, Timothy Jenkins, an alumnus and trustee of Howard, has written: "One can define the whole need for disproportioned treatment quite independently of the race of the people admitted. If you could insist, for instance, that the people who come into the professional schools make a contract for 10 or 20 year terms to serve low-income people, then you would have no need to be racially selective. But the fact of the matter is you could neither make nor enforce such a contract. Therefore, one must be more explicit in favoring those people who, in fact, are more likely to make a commitment to serve in that sector of the community that has the most acute medical, and public health needs for a long term. Viewed from that quasi-contractual perspective, independently of the race of the people involved, then I think you can have the proper focus on what needs to be done in the admission policies. Operating on that theory of a contract in its social sense, I think it is safe to say that there is an overwhelming disproportion of probability that black people will return by necessity of culture and custom to the black community to use their talents. It is not a philosophical position, it is a statistical position. It is justified not on the basis of the theory of differences of color, but on the practical necessities of the deprivation of peculiar enclaves within our society that we need to be concerned with a new racially-selective education." ("The Howard Professional School in a New Social Perspective," *Journal of the National Medical Association*, vol. 62 [1970], p. 167.)
56. *Journal of the American Medical Association*, vol. 222 (1972), p. 983.

The Black Doctor

1. In John C. Norman, ed., *Medicine in the Ghetto* (New York: Appleton, 1969), p. 182.
2. Dr. James Whittico, Jr., personal communication.
3. "Characteristics of Professional Workers," in *U.S. Census of Population: 1960* (Washington, D.C.: Bureau of the Census, 1964), Table 2 (PC2-7E).
4. M. Alfred Haynes, "Distribution of Black Physicians in the United States, 1967," *Journal of the American Medical Association*, vol. 210 (1969), p. 93; Leonard W. Johnson, Jr., "History of the Education of Negro Physicians," *Journal of Medical Education*, vol. 42 (1967), p. 444.
5. New York *Times*, April 8, 1973, p. 5.
6. Editorial, "Reservoirs of Compassion," *New England Journal of Medicine*, vol. 267 (1962), p. 940.
7. Johnson, pp. 444, 445. M. Montague Cobb, "A New Dawn in Medicine," *Ebony Magazine*, vol. 18 (1963), pp. 166–171.
8. *Statistical Abstract of the United States: 1968* (Washington, D.C.: Bureau of the Census, 1968), p. 67.
9. Haynes, "Distribution," p. 95.
10. *Ibid.*

11. *Ibid.*, pp. 93, 95.
12. "Selected Characteristics of the Members of the National Medical Association: Preliminary Findings," *Journal of the National Medical Association*, vol. 62 (1970), pp. 3, 4.
13. S. S. Goldwater, "The Extension of Hospital Privileges to All Practitioners of Medicine," *Journal of the American Medical Association*, vol. 84 (1925), pp. 933, 935.
14. Lawrence Greeley Brown, "Experience with Racial Attitudes of the Medical Profession in New Jersey," *Journal of the National Medical Association*, vol. 55 (1963), p. 66.
15. *Ibid.*, pp. 66–67.
16. Dietrich C. Reitzes, *Negroes in Medicine* (Cambridge, Mass.: Harvard University Press, 1958).
17. M. Alfred Haynes, "Problems Facing the Negro in Medicine Today," *Journal of the American Medical Association*, vol. 209 (1969), p. 1069.
18. See the five-part series in *Medical Tribune*, issues of October 10, 14, 17, 21, and 24, 1968.
19. *Journal of the National Medical Association*, vol. 59 (November 1967).
20. James L. Curtis, *Blacks, Medical Schools, and Society* (Ann Arbor: University of Michigan Press, 1971), p. 15.
21. *Ibid.*, p. 24.
22. *Skin and Allergy News*, vol. 3 (October 1972), p. 10.
23. Martin Luther King, Jr., *Why We Can't Wait* (New York: Harper, 1964), pp. 20ff.

Meeting the Challenge

1. A statement issued in October 1972, p. 1.
2. *New York Times*, August 8, 1971.
3. The material for this paragraph was taken mostly from *Proceedings: Conference–Workshop of Regional Medical Programs*, 2 vols. PHS Publication Nos. 1773–1774.
4. *American Medical News*, March 26, 1973, p. 8.
5. *An Evaluation of the Neighborhood Health Center Program* (Washington, D.C.: OEO, May 1972), 28 pp.
6. The facts reported here about Watts-Willowbrook were taken from a paper delivered by Rodney N. Powell, then director of the project, at a conference held in Portsmouth, New Hampshire, in June 1969. See "What Has Happened in the Watts-Willowbrook Program?" in John C. Norman, ed., *Medicine in the Ghetto* (New York: Appleton, 1969), pp. 73–86, quoted here by permission of the copyright holder, the Meredith Corporation.
7. Dr. Rodney Powell, personal communication.
8. See Dr. Joyce Lashof's report in *New York Academy of Medicine Bulletin*, vol. 44, no. 11 (November 1968), pp. 1363–1369.
9. *Ibid.*, pp. 1368–1369.
10. The material about Mound Bayou was reported in *Medical World News*, August 11, 1972, and March 16, 1973. Also see *Modern Medicine*, October 2, 1972, pp. 31–32.
11. For information about free clinics, see *Health Par Bulletin*, vol. 34 (October 1971); *Pediatric Herald*, November 24, 1971, p. 7; *California Medi-*

cine, vol. 116 (April 1972), pp. 106–111; *Journal of the American Medical Association*, vol. 220 (May and June 1972); and *Texas Medicine*, vol. 68 (February 1972), pp. 94–100.

12. Information for this section was taken from "Pilot City Health Center: 1972 Budget and Narrative," mimeographed, and from my personal knowledge of how the Center operates.

13. "Pilot City Health Center: 1972 Budget and Narrative," p. 65.

14. *Askov American*, December 7, 1972, guest editorial.

15. Health Professionals for Political Action, "National Health Insurance Position Paper," mimeographed.

Index

INDEX

Adams, William R., 75
AFDC program, 33, 95
Alabama, 60, 70
American Academy of General
    Practice, 74
American Academy of Pediatrics, 37,
    38
American Hospital Association, 72
American Indians, 4, 27, 55, 78
American Management Association, 62
American Medical Association (AMA):
    presidents of, 2, 81; and Head Start
    program, 37; discrimination against
    black doctors practiced by, 59, 69,
    74, 77–78, 112–113; recent atti-
    tudes of, 74, 79, 80–82, 113, 115;
    and relations with NMA, 77–80,
    113–114, 115; journal of, 78; policy
    of on health legislation, 79, 81, 85,
    86; 1971 resolution of House of
    Delegates of, 81; 1972 convention
    of, 81; Board of Trustees of, 81;
    Medicredit health insurance plan of,
    85, 86
American Public Health Association,
    92
Anemia, 33, 38
Appalachians, 12, 78
"Are Ghetto Physicians Welcome to
    the Mainstream of American Medi-
    cine?", 68
Aristotle, 1
Arkansas, 45, 70, 103
Arthritis, 14
Association of American Medical Col-
    leges, 48
Athens, Georgia, 17
Atlanta, 59
Australia, 31

Becker, E. Lowell, 47, 52

Bedford-Stuyvesant, Brooklyn, 13
Bellinger, Arnold C., 60–61
Beri-beri, 12
Bethel Synagogue, 95
Bingham Associates Fund, 87
Black child: life expectancy of, 7, 27;
    immunization of against contagious
    diseases, 10, 13, 32, 38, 41, 103; and
    "deprivation syndrome," 27, 41;
    value of comprehensive care for, 31,
    103–105, 114–115; effects of mal-
    nutrition on, 32–34; and mental ill-
    ness, 34; educational experience of,
    34–36, 38, 111. See also Head Start
    program; Infant mortality rates
Black dental students: number of, 61;
    recruitment of, 61–63; discrimina-
    tion against, 61–66 passim
Black doctors: number of, 43, 45, 63,
    66, 67, 69, 112; and discrimination
    in medical societies, 43, 59, 69, 74,
    76, 77–78, 112–113; specializations
    of, 43, 66, 71, 82, 123n55; geo-
    graphic distribution of, 56–58, 64–
    66, 70–71, 113; discrimination
    against, 56–59, 63–66, 68–83 pas-
    sim, 112–113; and hospital staff
    privileges, 57, 58, 59, 71–77 pas-
    sim, 112–113; and AMA, 59, 69, 74,
    77–78, 112–113; current outlook
    for, 77, 82–83, 114. See also Black
    medical students
Black medical students: discrimination
    against, 43–48, 49, 54–58, 111–112;
    medical schools attended by, 45–46,
    55, 112; performance on MCAT of,
    46–47, 49, 111; number of, 46, 66,
    69; recruitment of, 48–56; educa-
    tional background of, 49–51; and
    financial aid programs, 51–52, 53–
    54, 56, 58, 66, 80, 112; NMA aid to,

129